On (and Off) the Portuguese Way

Celtic Connections –
Galicia, Ireland and Everywhere

Roy Uprichard

The terms Portuguese Way or Camino Portugués refer to a series of ancient pilgrim paths from Portugal and Galicia to St James's shrine in Santiago de Compostela.

MAP OF IRELAND

MAP OF GALICIA

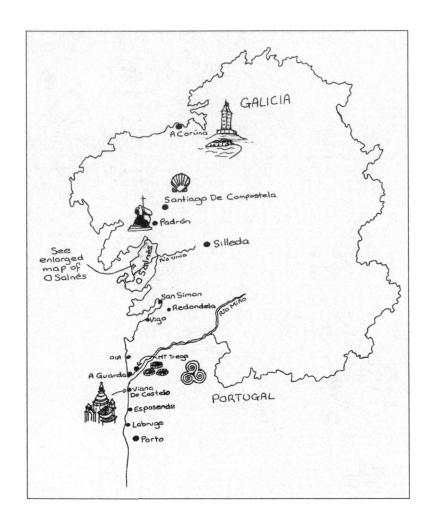

Map of O Salnés

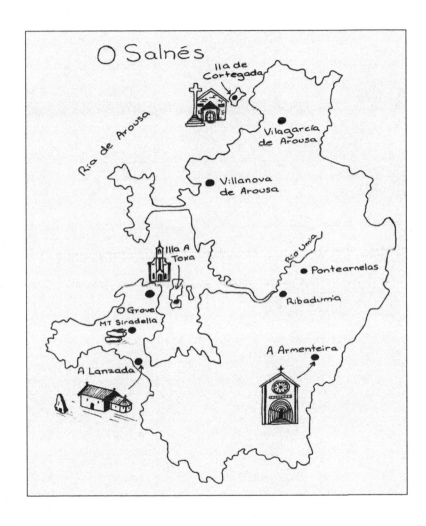

Table of Contents

Preface

The snapshot essays that follow draw from multiple walks and visits that took place between 2016 and 2019, with some names changed in privacy interests.

I offer these pen portraits hoping that they may inspire you on your own journeys of discovery – both at home and, when we can safely travel again, abroad.

Introduction

'If you can see your path laid out in front of you step-by-step, you know it's not your path. Your own path you make with every step you take. That's why it's your path.'

Joseph Campbell

Sometimes you long to journey and don't know why. The Germans named this as far-sickness, *Fernweh* (wanderlust).

So you trace the map lines from Porto to Santiago de Compostela, along the Camino Portugués Coastal, Central and Variante routes, relishing the names of unfamiliar places – like Labruge, Redondela or Armenteira.

On Camino, with our eyes so fixed on the goal of Santiago ahead, we often speed through places, landing only a glancing blow, gleaning only a sliver of their stories. How could it be otherwise? It's the nature of Pilgrimage – getting from here to there.

In 2016, I fell in love with the Portuguese route and its Spiritual Variant. Its pastoral paths, less crowded, more meditative, gave me what I longed for. And when you fall in love with places, they keep drawing you back. To say more.

I was lucky that I could indulge this passion through repeat journeys, to places that, like people, revealed themselves only slowly.

To walk the various Ways is to join a community of the imagination, one defined not by culture, language or skin tone, but by the stories we hear and tell each other – of our shared humanity.

These ones occur on the Atlantic's edge, threading the line between land and sea, or within sight of lough, ria or river. For it was water that brought us together, rather than kept us apart.

And with each walk or visit, more connections emerged – not only of a Celtic soul shared between Ireland and Galicia but something more. People and places *everywhere* becoming interconnected and braided together, deep-rooted in a shared Indo-European heritage and ancient Westward migrations.

With hindsight, it seems to me that the Camino might almost be a demonstration of or an active learning tutorial in Celtic Christian spirituality. Reconnecting us to primal memories, to the earth, the cycle of the seasons and our place in the cosmos; its reverence for nature resonant again, chiming with urgent ecological concerns; a spirituality that still has much to say. Its inclusive ethos a liberation from toxic religion with its fear of punishment by a capricious God.

But I knew little of this when I set off for Porto, to walk the Coastal Camino, to add it to the Central and Variante routes of the Camino Portugués.

A note on the seven sections
Section 1: On and Off the Coastal Camino sees boardwalk beginnings, the extraordinary in the ordinary and mountain-top moments of wonder. Plus, evidence of historical, cultural connections between Galicia and Ireland.

Section 2: Home in Ireland sees me follow up those connections and learn of recent discoveries unearthing deep pilgrimage roots and a journey to the light. A workshop on Celtic Christianity and some family-tree research make things personal. The breadcrumb trail leads to a Sacred Space and a legend that later appears elsewhere.

Section 3: Places off the Spiritual Variant shows that even when a Camino seems to go wrong, it can lead to places of great beauty, rich in culture and history. Places like the O Salnes region, which cradles a striking resonance with an Irish origin myth.

Section 4: Seaways – The First Celtic Camino sees me propelled north to A Corunna and then County Kerry – following mythic journeys and arrivals. To where avid keepers of the past found a way to weave paradox into harmony. As a fellow pilgrim said, 'Sometimes places are like things. One leads to another'.

Section 5: On the Central Route is set in the Redondela region and tells of how a family, torn apart by war, found dignity in compassion. And how a community has sought to remember and redeem the past.

Section 6: On the Spiritual Variant takes me back to familiar paths explored in my previous book *Stone and Water* and further into shared myths and legends. In Armenteira, a conversation reveals more of its rich history and an inclusive spirituality that chimes with Irish Celtic tradition.

In this place where life flows all around, I recall a River Pilgrimage from the source of the Umia to the Ria de Arousa – with its attendant hopes of healing dreams. The section ends with two Irishmen getting very wet wading across to an abandoned island with the largest laurel forest in Europe, and its own extraordinary story.

Section 7: Thoughts from Home and Abroad offers a reflection on a beloved river and a remembrance recall of an unforgettable encounter on Padron's Mount Santiaguinio. A C.S. Lewis linkage to Pilgrimage leads to mid-winter observations on the Advent season and the difficulty of bringing the Camino experience home. Yet, memories that enrich rise as I go forward to an altar rail on Christmas Eve.

A short Afterword sees me revisit Nendrum as the Covid pandemic takes hold, yet somehow find hope midst rising anxiety.

If I ever write another book, it would need to say much more on how to bring the Camino experience home and embed it in our lives.

SECTION 1
On (and off) the Coastal Camino

CHAPTER 1

Labruge

Only yesterday I walked County Down's smooth sands, through still air, the water as if set. Tonight, ten miles north of Porto, whitecaps rush the rocks in Bardic moments – 'like minutes that hasten to their end ... each changing place with that which goes before...' (Shakespeare's Sonnet 60)

Nothing new, this draw to shorelines. It dates back to childhood summers on the Antrim Coast, where I'd peer past Ailsa Craig to white-stone cottages sewn into Kintyre's green hillsides.

But a child's imagination reached further, fed by library book tales of ancient Greece and Dark Ages Ireland; of Jason and Ulysses; of Brendan voyaging or Columba setting coracles in motion; to Iona, and Lindisfarne. And me there with them. All the possibility before one, the past ever-present on unchanging seas; the tang of salt already seeped deep into clothes and bones.

But tonight a different coastal calling, drawing me along board-walks and over rocks. Weaving a line through places on the edge.

Any excuse. Though this time, because beyond the gulls hung in the wind, Legend says St James once sailed past – a carpenter's cousin drawn back from the Mediterranean to Iberia's Atlantic waters; the storm of this 'Son of Thunder' not yet spent.

The story of his return, his *Translatio*, says it was the very same Hand of God: 'Manu Domini Gubernante' that hovered over the Genesis waters of chaos, that piloted this hero home across a seascape, its nature unchanging, its portraiture constant. Though it records no trace of our journeys except brief wakes, yet the James story *did* leave its mark – of myth carved deep on the ocean of our imagination, inspiring millions of others to journey.

I stop for a moment at the water's edge. He'd be at home here. This fisherman apostle. Amongst the salt of the earth, the people of the sea acquainted with heartbreak and danger, who ploughed the ocean with their calloused hands – their sardines tonight charcoal smoking. He too knew what it was like to be called to Masefield's vagrant gipsy life.

Again, I'm caught in his wake listening for echoes from beyond the bar. Cast like bread upon the waters, he was found after many days. Good comes back to you, Wisdom says, or storms hit, and you never know why.

I arrive at the Casa. The owner is polite, professional. He's seen it all many times: the nervous excitement of the night before – as if the walk might yield answers to myriad questions, some reveal waiting as we walk toward our best thoughts and away from our worst.

Golden Hour. The sun-blazed houses turn from ochre to pink. A rib of cloud. A ghost moon low in the East. And in my room, solitude's soundtrack: the howl of tyres on granite cobblestone. Then the restless roaring sea.

Labruge – Boardwalk beginnings

CHAPTER 2

Meithal in Malafia

Each morning, the boardwalk creaks and sways to the slap of feet as we gather each other up like strays into the community of the Road.

Gerry from Dublin, 'Just had to get back.' His Camino Frances two years ago, 'was full of special people and places.'

He finds it strange, that as a member of the Irish Humanist Society he's drawn to the Camino. 'I suppose religion is still lodged in us somewhere.'

He walks with Marie from Galloway on the Scottish coast, which is across the Irish Sea from where I now live. Last year, within three months, she lost her mother, grandmother and best friend and walked numb, to Santiago. 'It was only on the coast, at Finisterre, that all the emotion came. 'It took the sea. I wasn't ready until then.'

It seems that our own fragile bodies of water often draw comfort from other immense and durable ones – of sea and river.

'But there's still work in the walking,' she says with a wry smile, 'if we're minded to shed excess baggage.'

This year, she'll keep the sea in sight.

Set for Viana do Castelo, we climb inland through cone-thick pines leaving behind the hush of grey sea far below. Outside a sawmill, the scent of woodsmoke drifts marijuana-sweet. Blue-tiled images of an artisan Jesus carrying an armful of logs he has just sawn to his workshop, to be made into tables and chairs, as Mary sews.

The village of San Marinhas, with its cobblestone streets, displays lavish gardens with Marian figurines set amidst a riot of roses. My morning reading has counselled finding the extraordinary in the ordinary.

'So much beauty here,' Gerry says. 'Perhaps we notice it more in Autumn when it's starting to fade. Scarcity value, someone said.'

I stop at a coffee shop sign, 300 metres off the track.

'Scarce enough,' I say. 'Shall we?'

We follow a group, passing a vivid young sandstone St James as he strides forward. At the Quinta da Malafaia the tables are out, but the shutters stay down.

The sandstone St James at Malafia

Shoulders sag, but we join others and sit there anyway, everyone soon rustling through packs in search of remaining snacks. A Norwegian family passes round a large packet of biscuits, an American couple offers sweet cakes. Marie has Pastels de Nata, and Gerry and I have Naranja. The mood lightens.

'This is why I love the Camino,' Gerry announces, 'the sense of community, with no-one in command. It reminds me of an Irish word: *Meitheal*, meaning a gathering or assembly. Like when neighbours rally to save a crop or repair a barn – some sense of *Oneness*.'

Marie says, 'We have a similar word in Scotland: Neighbouring.'

I tell them I've read of this in an article by the Camino Society of Ireland's Turlough O'Donnell, who sees how the Camino can be a co-operative endeavour … with each of us part of something bigger.

Perhaps a certain '*Meitha*l' Oneness echoes along every Camino path, with our pooled stories becoming somehow greater than the sum of them all. I've often wondered what it felt like to be part of a whole mobilised wartime society drawn together in a single purpose…

Such reflections flutter away as the cafe's door opens, and the owner emerges. We look up sheepishly, expecting to be told off and shooed along.

Instead, he greets us and apologises for their holiday closure. 'But – I will make coffee for you.'

Broad smiles. Never have Cafe Con Leches and Espressos tasted so good. We get our wallets out but he refuses.

'No, no. It's an offering. For your Camino.'

The extraordinary in the ordinary again!

We walk on, and I mention the fascination the Camino has for a friend back home. 'He advises that we pause each day and reflect; see where the meaning's been; where something bigger was active in the little things.'

Gerry nods and tells of a framed photo he has of Charlie Brown sitting with Snoopy, toasting marshmallows in front of a roaring fire. Its caption says, 'Someday you'll look back and realise the little things were the big things.'

He's right. Like a garden in Autumn. A forest path by a river. Or a coffee in Quinta da Malafaia.

Mount Trega (A Guarda)

For two days now, rising in the distance and glimpsed through the mist, Mount Trega guards Galicia. I'm drawn to it, but don't know why. In Caminha, we're in its shadow cast.

Over dinner, the talk turns serious, to Irish wakes, and confession. One at our table confessed to a Portuguese Priest with no English. 'He didn't know what I was admitting…'

Marie shrugs and adds, 'I just wanted the blessing, I don't know why. At home, I never go.'

Perhaps it's because the primal is here, just across the Rio Minho.

In the morning, the ferry powers through breeze and waves, seagulls wheeling in its wake as it reaches the lee of Trega.

I stop for a moment at a sign pointing uphill to the remains of a Celtic settlement. When I ask the others, 'You interested?' They shake their heads.

'Looks a bit steep,' Gerry says. 'I like the flatter mountains now.' I know what he means and say I'll catch up with them later.

It *is* steep – steep as the Route Napoleon out of St-Jean. But after a few hundred metres, a car slows and a man shouts, 'Hey, Amigo. You like a lift?'

Very much so, I tell him, and climb into his battered Seat.

Bright eyes in a weather-beaten face. Thick black hair. Stippled stubble.

A strong right hand grips mine as his left rebounds from his sternum. 'I am Sergio, the Comandante of this site.' His head tilts backwards as he asks, 'Are you inglés?'

No, I tell him. 'Irlandés. Desde Irlanda del Norte.'

He nods, pleased with this response. Last year he was in Kerry, visiting relatives, mentions a name, then asks, 'Do you know them?'

I say, 'I don't think so,' and we stutter off, leaving a cloud of exhaust smoke hung in the air like squid-black ink. A startled motorcyclist is consumed for a moment, before he emerges wide-eyed to race past.

The Seat also builds speed – too much speed, coiling around the mountain, intent on its summit 300 metres above.

Tyres screech. Spirals tighten. Wind whistles through open windows. My right hand reaches for the roof bar as panoramas carousel past: now the Miño estuary, then the Portuguese, then the Galician coast. My grip relaxes as our climb finally unravels before a museum.

Sergio has saved me a forty-minute hike. Even better, he now shepherds me inside and introduces me to the museum's manager, Antonio Castro – with the request that he explains all to me 'En inglés.'[1]

Then Sergio's off into animated conversations, backslapping shopkeepers like an election candidate working the room.

Behind the wide-smiling Antonio hangs a wall-map decorated with dots designating Castro sites in Northern Portugal and along the Galician coast.

Trega, he tells me, is the most important in North-West Spain, *and* the best-preserved. 'Celtic culture is a thing of pride to us Galicians.'

He shows me his screensaver – a photograph of a triple spiral Triskelion marked into the ground at Celta de Vigo football stadium.[2]

'The power of three was central to Celts, indicating that all life is interconnected,' he explains.

'There was already a settlement here when the Romans came over 2000 years ago. Its hoard is the largest ever recovered.'

He ushers me to an exhibition space. I walk through darkened rooms full of signature silver torques and backlit golden urns lovingly laid on black velvet. To linger over ornate brooches with interwoven patterns and circular swirls. Some have the interconnecting tri-spirals I've seen somewhere before. Then remember where: in a magazine article about Ireland's Newgrange Neolithic site in the Boyne Valley in Co. Meath and their Winter Solstice rituals. Similar tri-spirals are on its entrance stone to a Passage Grave from five millennia ago. A place older than Stonehenge, older than any Celtic Age. And only eighty miles away from where I live.[3]

I make a vow to visit it when I get home.

CHAPTER 4

Celts, Seaborne Saints and a Pauline Protegee

The museum circuit returns me to the front desk. Now Antonio walks me out to the Mount Facho peak with its view of the twenty-hectare Citania (village) below, once replete with reservoir, water channels, and paved streets, catering for 5,000 residents.

Like Celts everywhere, they had been efficient farmers, growing wheat, barley, oats, and millet.

They even boasted artists, potters, and smiths, crafted jewellery and woven woollen garments in a complex division of labour between subsistence and trade.[4]

Mount Trega had been a vital stopover point, a crucial link in the Punic commercial route north from Cádiz trading tin, leather and slaves. Then the Romans came, saw and conquered. They laid roads and rewrote rules and histories, inducing amnesia of the sea lanes, the quickest means of connecting Atlantic peoples.

Today Mt. Trega looks as if some Galician Finn McCool had thrown hundreds of stone coits over the hillside. The pattern of the dwellings also indicate a caste system, with some spaciously spread out on the higher ground, others tight-packed below.

Antonio hands me a leaflet showing photographs of a few 'Showhouses' which have been restored to their original condition:

six feet of circular stone topped by conical straw, their door lintels richly decorated with something confirming caste. Swas-tika's – the Indo-European symbol of good fortune.[5]

Some of the Citania's remains

His phone buzzes to summon him back to the museum. I thank him, lean into the wind and walk to the viewpoint's edge.

To the North, beyond the San Francisco peak, hang-glider views vie for attention. But my eyes are drawn inland, along the Río Miño, to where, far beyond sight, the río rises north of Lugo. In the stillness of the Meira mountains, it gathers itself to flow 340 kilometres before merging again with the Atlantic.

From Caminha, the ferry launches out once more, also leaning into the wind, battling the current, its wake forming an arc of white scribed on blue.

It was on the island of A Insua, at the río's estuary's confluence, according to a leaflet, that the Franciscan religious order arrived in the sixteenth-century.

The resonance of story and place recalls Strangford Lough in Co. Down, which has its own ferry crossing, and which received St Patrick's landing at Saul, from where he spread his *Godspel*, his Good News.

Seaborne saints like James and Patrick shared the spirit of Francis, living in simplicity and vowed to service. All arrived in lavishly fertile estuary places where fresh and saltwater merge. It was similar conditions which inspired the Greek Myth (adopted by the Celts) that the world arose when the freshwater stream Tethys mingled with the saltwater sea Okeanos.

W.B. Yeats thought that the water of the seas and lakes, mist and rain had 'all but made the Irish in its image'.

And perhaps not only the Irish.

This place has such a presence, a peace about it. You know the Camino involves hard yards and destinations, but it also offers moments like these: not rushing between places but dwelling on the places in between – slowing down for unexpected moments of connection.

I talk with Americans and Spaniards, some with distant origins in Cork or Donegal who plan to return and find their roots, their home places. Our accents are different, yet we are enriched like the estuary in encountering the other.

* * *

Descending to another stone cross, I find this one dedicated to Saint Francis outside a shrine to Santa Tecla, an early disciple of St. Paul.

Though more revered in the Syrian and Greek Eastern Orthodox Church, Santa Tecla has another outpost on the Catalan Coast as patron saint of Tarragona since the fourteenth-century.[6]

An arched doorway brings me into her twelfth-century hermitage where family groups have already gathered.

At the front stands a life-sized figurine of Tecla, her dark tresses flowing over her shoulders, red cloak and white surplice. Opposite, an image of la Virgen del Carmen, the Virgin of the Sea. Then a portrait of St Paul.

A guide fleshes out Tecla's legend. Born in A.D. 30 to a noble family in Iconium (now south-west Turkey), she was so entranced by St. Paul's three days of preaching when he visited there that she abandoned both fiancé and family, followed him to Antioch and dedicated herself to an itinerant, celibate life.[7]

The Eastern Orthodox Church considered her 'equal to the apostles'. A patron of female empowerment, to whom numerous shrines in Syria and forty-two churches in Lebanon are dedicated. Some repeat, 'Cuarenta y dos' to each other (42 in English). Reassured and reminded that they are not alone in their devotion.

21

We are told that as her feast day of 24th September approaches, her power to answer prayers of petition increases. Her areas of particular influence are problems of the head and heart.

After the presentation, the group files to the front, lights candles, slot coins into a wooden box and collects Tecla prayer cards. One woman presses a card to the forehead of her pew-seated husband, before rubbing it over his chest, remarking, 'Need a big miracle here.'

He looks up and smiles as others laugh.

Under Tecla's image lie rows of children's shoes in gratitude for past healings. There, a young couple embrace. He whispers something. Her lips move in reply, in this place of whispers to another world, before both reach for Tecla's touch-smoothed toes.

* * *

Out again in the bright sunshine, hundreds of steps wind up to the radio tower while others descend steeply past a *Vía Crucis*, a Way of the Cross – fourteen Stations of twelve-feet-high stone crosses liberated from Church Nave to a hillside. But fittingly, these are Celtic stone crosses, their superimposed circles once symbolising the sun's circuit or the seasons turning, later repurposed to represent eternal life; their solid sun-dial faces are surrounded by Celtic knots and weaves, a sacred geometry without beginning or end.

Celtic stations

I complete this way of the cross and sit for a while, gazing longingly gazing back up at Trega. And as I'm reminded of a Chesterton quote, that there's a road from the eye to the heart that doesn't go through the mind, neurons fire then wire together laying down a pathway of connection with this place.

Eventually I check my watch. And double-take. Four hours since Sergio stopping. It seems like only one.

Chapter 5

Oia

Ahead, A Guarda's sun-washed squares lead me in turn to family-friendly coves, past igneous rock, and along a path through pine and eucalyptus.

The others are ahead but, suddenly tired, I'm drawn to descend through Oia's narrowing streets, past ancient casement windowed houses of stone, to a room with a view over both a crescent bay – *and* the weathered sandstone of a Cistercian Monastery where wind-blown samphire has lodged like prayers in a wailing sea wall.

Another Golden Hour, when light glows through crimson bordered water-colour clouds.

The tide is high as paddle boarders begin a final circuit of a gold-rippled bay – sun kissing sea on a day of wonders.

Then a slow spill of stars, such as I've never seen before.

I leave the shutters open. It's been years since I fell asleep to the relentless roar of surf. It takes me back to childhood summers spent in sight of a village harbour, counting the trawlers out and back, casting nets or lifting lobster pots. When we'd be sung safe to sleep by an evensong soundtrack of wind-whipped wire hawsers ching-ringing morse on metal masts. With all possibility before us.

Even then, it was only by County Down's Irish Sea (not the Atlantic Ocean), where the family gathered, where laughter rose, and seafaring uncles told tales of their Mediterranean fog of war, and of other wild men, tonsured and cassocked, setting coracles in motion to Iona or Lindisfarne.

But tonight, I also pictured the people of Trega amidst their domestic routines high over sea and river, or eating evening meals by hearth-light, listening to stories of star-fields where the ancestors might be gathered; or of the womb of the earth, where the sun god rebirthed each and every morning. And realise how some of these tales were also nurtured in the Boyne valley.

When I get home, I'll visit Newgrange and look closely at their tri-spirals and solstice rituals; their similar tryst with the sleeping sun god.

What was it Marie had said? 'Sometimes places are like things – one leads to another.'

SECTION 2
Home in Ireland

CHAPTER 6

Newgrange, or, The Bru na Boinne

It might be a March morning when you visit Newgrange. On the first tour of the day, the air razor-sharp as wisps of birdsong drift from pared branches. Clouds parting; sky towering. The low sun over rich pastures illumines the meandering river as it loops around the Bru na Boinne (the Palace of the Boyne).

But it's the cairn that dominates – the last link in a long evolution. Seeded from Brittany and Iberia, its giant mound on high ground covers a Passage Grave. The huge stones in this burial chamber align to receive a single winter solstice sunbeam.

The quartz and granite facade glows, still evoking wonder. We stop before the entrance stone, carved with the same Tri-spirals as atop Mount Trega in Galicia. Are they intended as a map of the valley and its river? The clockwise and anticlockwise spirals representing summer and winter? Or hallucinogenic journeys?

We just don't know.

You have to bow to enter the nineteen-metre passageway, long, narrow, narrowing – as if you're peering down a portal to the past. At times, it's claustrophobic and you turn sideways, crouch, squeeze past, then press on to release and relief in a cross-shaped chamber stretched seven metres under a corbelled roof.

Newgrange entrance stone and roof box

Another Tri-Spiral carving, and Basin Stones in East and West alcoves, where the ancestors' ashes once lay laced with jewellery, amber beads and blood-red ochre. All waiting for the light, under 200,000 tons of earth and stone laboured and levered into place by the first farmers, a community mobilised to monumental endeavour, transforming Space into Place. Even so, they still saw themselves as part of nature, not separate from it.

You wonder if they were like bees amidst a hive of activity serving the Queen, without knowledge of the bigger picture or exact reason why. For all was communal then, all for tribe or clan, with little sense of individual consciousness. We only occasionally see a trace of it now, in the collective grief of a Diana moment, or joy midst a sporting event, breaking like waves over a crowd – when the barriers between us fleetingly dissolve. Into the 'Oneness' that lingers in the consciousness of rural communities, echoing not only in Malafia.

Somebody whispers, 'If you want to know what a people really believe, look at their rituals; what they do, not what they say.' If so, Newgrange was this people's sermon in stone.

The guide informs you that the Solstice display can be artificially replicated. Clustered together, you watch bulbs dim, waiting, as people did 5,000 years ago, for the first ray to penetrate the roof-box.

Suddenly a pencil of pale ambient sunlight arrives and moves down the passageway becoming a beam. In what you begin to believe was a study of light, for a moment not scattered but a fragment of its force captured and concentrated, distilled for a close quarter encounter with a living entity that warmed the earth, coaxed forth life. Though we can't see light, only by it, we're still drawn by beams.

Yet, confected or real, the radiance retreats and you walk out to sun.

A robin trills. The river glints silver. A heron stands serene. Seeds stir underground.

Chapter 7

Unearthing a Pilgrimage to Light

Walking the adjoining road later, I visualise crowds assembled on a long-ago midwinter's eve – at this site converted from shamanic training centre to a place of public spectacle, from the few to the many. A silver mace-head gleams in the torchlight and leads elders and peoples along avenues of approach. To drama, shock, then the awe of the cairn's reveal, site for feasting, prayer and ecstatic dance that precedes silent waiting for the sun.

It seems that the Boyne Valley sites offered something remarkably like Pilgrimage. To the light.

Something I checked later with Professor Geraldine Stout, Chief Archaeologist of the Newgrange excavations.

'Definitely,' Geraldine said, 'One had to bow one's head to enter Passage Graves, a mark of respect for the deity and the ancestors. Only then did the tomb open up. Even their construction and alignment would indicate these were places to which pilgrims travelled at solstice times.'

Do we know of the numbers of Newgrange visitors?

'We can't accurately estimate that. But they came from beyond the immediate locality. Some of the artefacts found during excavation include Antrim and Orkney flint.

'We also uncovered stone lamps and stone food and water bowls used by pilgrims visiting sacred landscapes and monuments.'

In 2018, fresh excavations brought new finds from the Late Neolithic (Stone Age): large holding areas for significant numbers of pilgrims came to light; a monumentalised avenue of approach, and pits full of animal bones, evidencing lots of feasting.

'Perhaps it responded to growing demand?' I mused.

'Perhaps. Newgrange becomes even more monumental as the Neolithic progresses,' she points out. 'Art becomes more decorative, with carvings at entrances, idols and stones placed outside to enhance the approach. The same in Knowth, another passage grave in the Bru na Boinne complex.'

I wondered if these sacred journeys, which bonded communities, partly accounted for the continuing appeal of Pilgrimage. Or explained why so many Irish people are now drawn to return to places where this type of Pilgrimage may have begun.

'It's certainly deeply ingrained in us,' she said.

'The passage tombs in Galicia are older than Ireland's and also occur mostly on or near the coast. We seem to have followed their example. Perhaps that's why some people are curious as to their own possible Galician origins.[8]

'There are many clear connections,' she continued. 'The tombs at Forno Dos Mouros (also used at solstice times), their angular wall art, saw-tooth crenelles and pendants with similar criss-cross symbols carvings correspond exactly to symbols on Irish tombs. So do their fern-like motifs. And scallop shells, usually associated with Galicia, have been found in Irish tombs.

'But such similarities are not confined to Ireland and Galicia. It's much wider. I could document similar instances that link the Boyne and places in Brittany.'[9]

* * *

It was slowly becoming clearer that Pilgrimage was not just the story of a single people journeying to their special places, but of peoples and places *everywhere* becoming interconnected and braided together.

Professor Stout passed me a map showing clusters of passage tombs and megalithic art that had likely originated in Gaul and spread out along the Atlantic coastal areas: Galicia, Iberia, Ireland and as far as Orkney.

These peoples were expert sailors, she stressed. The ocean, central to their story, enabled greater population and cultural mobility than was previously realised ... connecting, not dividing, as had been assumed.

Sociologist Owen Barfield, sometimes known as 'The Last Inkling,' given his longevity, speculated that human consciousness evolves over time, from the collective of the tribe or clan, to individuals. This led to the rejection of myth in favour of more rational thought.

But he notes a later tendency to reconnect with myth and ritual – through choice, not compulsion, as we re-engage with wonder.

Perhaps when ancient rituals re-emerge, they signal again the centrality of community and our interdependence. For while all nations are effectively 'Imagined Communities,' there may also be 'Communities of the Imagination,' cross-cutting national and cultural boundaries to create a new identity. Some of them clothed in temporary Pilgrim garments walking along myriad paths that vein not only Spain, Portugal or France, but every continent.

Next summer I'll rejoin this community, walking again north from Porto. And find fresh direction even when things seem to go wrong.

CHAPTER 8

A Celtic Christianity Workshop and a Dream

An email pinged in the top corner of my lap-top. From the Corrymeela Community on the North Antrim coastline, advertising a workshop on Celtic Christian Spirituality. I immediately responded. Another breadcrumb on the trail, perhaps.

Descending into Corrymeela's Croi, a circular meeting space set into the earth, Anglican minister Grace Clunie told the story of a pre-Roman Celtic world that once stretched across a swathe of Europe, east from Anatolia, then through Roman opposition shrank to a 'Celtic Fringe', of Brittany, Cornwall, Wales, Scotland, Ireland and Galicia.

But something distinctive happened in Ireland. For it was the dry winds of the eastern Desert Fathers and the Egyptian Coptic Church that scattered the exotic seeds of belief that planted its church. Seeds borne via Gaul and St Martin of Tours, where many Irish priests studied. Resulting in a marriage of Eastern Monasticism and Celtic Spirituality.

Its core tenets? A close relationship with all of creation; the presence of the Divine in all things. Therefore all of life was sacred, with reverence for Journey, Pilgrimage, and Creativity, with Heaven, the Otherworld ever proximate, only 'three feet away'.

Some kinaesthetic learning followed. Grace asked each person to take four coloured strands of wool, of which one had to be gold, and weave them into a wristband.

Irritated, as my clunky fingers grappled fine strands, I had to ask a woman beside me for help.

'Do you have a daughter?' she queried.

I nodded. 'All grown up now.'

'Did she ever ask you to put her hair into a French Plait?'

'Yes. Though it's been a while.'

I watched as she deftly lapped strands one over another, before passing them back for me to complete.

As we worked, Grace told a story:

In the creation poem of Genesis, Chapter one, God said seven times, over each layer of creation, 'it was good.' All things were good.

That was our beginning. And this sacred image remains at the core of our being. Everything else has to be read in the light of that fact – even our wrong turns.

In some Celtic communities, a belief existed that royal garments were woven through with a thread of gold. If that thread was removed, the whole garment would unravel. And so it is, also, for us.

Many early Celtic Christians believed that the image of God is woven into the very fabric of our being. The very life of God, the golden strand running through us.

She paused a moment for emphasis: 'Therefore, we may believe that we are sacred not because we belong to the right church, believe the right things, or pray in the right way. We are sacred *because we have been born.*'

Afterwards, I told her that I'd never heard this before.

She was unsurprised. 'It's rarely spoken of in this culture.' One, it seemed to me, defined by rival gatekeepers of the divine: Protestant and Roman Catholic, with their competing claims to a monopoly on truth and a focus on humanity as intrinsically sinful, fallen.

I told her of a long-forgotten dream I'd had as an enthusiastic eighteen-year-old evangelical convert.

In it, I stand at the base of an enormous stone cross, peering upwards to a starlit sky. The cross seems to stretch forever into the night as if it were True North, the very axis around which the universe spun. But it is a Celtic cross, deeply engraved with spirals, knots and weaves.

'It's strange,' I said, 'Things Celtic were not part of my Methodist family's tradition.'

She spoke softly, saying, 'You need to pay attention to that.'

She asks, 'Where's home for you?'.

I tell her Bangor, Co. Down.

'Not far from Nendrum then,' she muses.

'Where?'

'Just passed Comber, on Mahee island in Strangford Lough. It's the remains of a monastic settlement. You should go there.'

I wonder why, my face says.

'You'll see. It's a place I often went to, to pray when I lived close by. It has a presence about it.'

Then we talked a little about the Camino. Me telling her how so many of us felt we lived more intensely there, being often moved to tears yet not knowing why.

I echoed my earlier question to Geraldine Stout, wondering if all our walking is sparked by something deep in our nature, from shared memories of an earlier common ritual we are now re-enacting?

Grace nodded a 'yes.' And confirmed that when something ancient re-emerges into the culture, it needs to be taken seriously. 'Journeys on foot through nature connect us with mystery again. And it's no accident that some Celtic Crosses, like the one on Iona, are double-sided: Bible scenes on one; Nature images on the other. What they called the Two Books of God.'

Perhaps, on Camino, we read both.[10]

CHAPTER 9

Inner Light

I lifted a leaflet as I left and read that daily worship in the Croí is a thirty-minute 'Quaker-style,' silent reflection, with a short liturgy at the end. Something else to which I felt drawn.

Perhaps another journey began that day – this time inside the tent of belief, towards a more inclusive perspective, and one closer to my heart than I'd realised. Because shortly after, when researching my family history in the Public Records Office, more unexpected connections emerged.

Documents confirmed that my father's ancestors had been part of a seventeenth-century migration from the Celtic heartlands of Wales to the northern part of Ireland. And that many of them were Quakers fleeing persecution who established assemblies in Mid-Ulster – where their belief that there was, 'That of God in everyone, therefore all were equal,' practically echoed Celtic spirituality.

They'd gather to, 'centre down,' rather like in 'Mindfulness' practice, to await that 'inner light that illuminates the soul of all people: the Logos, the true Word that lights everyone who comes into the world.' One wrote that, 'It's in the waiting for silence to fall that we find stillness inside.' Critics levelled the charge that they abolished the clergy; but they answered, rather, that they'd abolished the laity.

It seems my father's fathers, then, came to Northern Ireland hard-wired for silence and reflection. But after a time some began to see their identity rather as transplanted, chosen 'insiders', becoming imaginary Jews in a land of promise. Whereas other, Catholic Celts were then deemed 'outsiders', designated as Philistines to be reduced to, 'hewers of wood and carriers of water'.

Captured by the power of angry voices and the sound of shoulder-strapped drums on summer mornings – sheep were separated from goats, into *them* and *us*. Them *or* us.

CHAPTER 10

Nendrum

Mayday morning. I'm driving through fertile farmland fringed by oyster beds, set for the upper reaches of Strangford Lough in County Down, and the tidal island of Mahee, where Nendrum's monastic remains linger still.

Its origins can be traced back to the fifth century and a direct link to St Patrick, which prompted a monastery's founding, an island naming. Newly arrived, Patrick met and baptised the swineherd Mo-Choi, (pronounced Mo-hee) and later ordained him as Ireland's first Bishop. (Both of them swineherds, the resonance with the Prodigal Son story writ large.)

Blackbird, robin and wren spill birdsong from ash trees, bursting into brilliance onto Nendrum's three circular limestone walls; Cashel walls that were once designated areas for agriculture and industry, scriptorium and cell. And at its heart, a sacred church space.

My hand traces the top of the middle wall. To where a big fat bee hovers by a bench and a scribed message announces that Liz and Nikita were 'very happy here today' last year, also on Mayday.

I sit on their bench and think back further to Nendrum's origin myth. Mo-Choi was cutting wattles for a church he planned to build on an island when he heard beautiful birdsong. It came falling from a bird, that sang and talked, sitting on a blackthorn and it gave Mo-Choi an assurance that his labour would be blest.

43

Remains of the monastery's church

He listens, enthralled, for what seemed like an hour of profound peace until the birdsong ceased. He returns with his wattles to continue building but finds the church complete. On a tidal island, on a setting marshalled as metaphor (in contact with the mainland for only half the day) – symbolic bridge between this and the Otherworld, with one foot in each. A stranger he questions informs him that the church had been dedicated to St Mo-Choi, who disappeared 300 years earlier.[11]

I try to imagine Nendrum at the height of its influence, Bishop Cronan in charge, the Bell Tower tolling the hours. Scriptorium quills are set down. The ring of hammers on steel ceases, for cowled monks to process clockwise from the bottom of the hill, to *their* Holy of Holies: a wooden church where they would also mediate between known and unknown, tangible and intangible.

Though the bell tower has been long silenced, the place still oozed presence. Grace was right.[12]

The archeologist Thomas McErlean, of the University of Ulster, told me that Mo-Choi had churches dedicated to him locally and in Donegal and at Whithorn in Scotland. His feast day of June 23rd, (close to the mid-summer solstice) is in common with St John, underlining the importance of John's gospel to Celtic theologians and to the Irish church. In the seventh century, Nendrum was an important place of Pilgrimage – when the independence of the British and Irish Celtic Church in Britain and Ireland became a contentious issue with Rome.

The bishops and abbots of the Irish church, (including Cronan) received a letter from Pope John IV reproaching them for their 'incorrect' dating of Easter and the cut of their overly Druidic monastic tonsure – shaved in front and long at the back.

But the Pope's real grievance was their overt sympathy with the proscribed teachings of the Welsh theologian Pelagius. His inclusive theology, which underlined the essential goodness of human nature and denied original sin, as well as his openness to native Celtic spirituality and its intimacy with Nature, were deemed by Rome as dangerous and rebellious. An affront to Augustinian orthodoxy. In a tussle of centralised structure and control versus the Wild Goose wind of the Spirit and of mystery.

The monks eventually lost that battle but won the war when, generations later, Quantum Physics and Neuroscience vindicated their insights that had fallen foul of Rome. Thanks to Carl Jung and others, the Celtic sense of connection, their early conviction that we all are interconnected, braided together for good or ill, now rates as accepted wisdom.

Something stirs the teal on the opposite shore and brings me back to the present. They catapult past so close I hear their murmuring wings. And, higher still, something like giant gossamer wings tinted dragonfly indigo, followed by a microlight's whine.

I stood and looked south, to Iberia and Portugal, where another season of Camino walking had already begun, to where I planned once more to walk north from Porto. Then I drove across the causeway, from one world back to another.

Section 3

Places Off the Spiritual Variant

*Sometimes when you get ill and can't finish a Camino
the journey leads you elsewhere …*

CHAPTER 11

Santiago Station and Centro Médico

A train full of pilgrims study maps of Santiago, satisfied that their walk is over. Mine, by contrast, remains incomplete.

The train slows. Everything slows to surreal. Lines of people pour onto platforms; new queues board. Our comings and goings, our stories breathed in and out, the lifeblood, the oxygen of this city-state, its conceit maybe, that it, not the pilgrims, is special.

I've seen so many come to try on a new hat, new shirt, twirl an old stick in a new way (somewhere between Chaplinesque and Billyboy) as they skip over the smooth-stone Golden Square to then set out again to catch their train home from another Mount Olympus.

This place of sandstone glistening, colonnades and cloister walks, yet tied to earth only lightly, seems as if at any moment it might slip its moorings and drift off on a westerly, lost in its own myth-making.

* * *

Perhaps I'm a little delirious, dizzily walking uphill to Centro Médico, (equivalent of Accident and Emergency). I make the mistake of asking the receptionist, '¿*Habla Ingles*' (Do you speak English?)' The English are not always popular here and even though I live in Northern Ireland, it's a matter of guilt by association.

49

He shakes his head and expels an angry 'No.'

I try to explain my symptoms, but he's only interested in my name, EHIC card and passport, before consigning me with a wave to the waiting room.

An hour later, softened, he stares from my backpack on the floor to me, leaves his desk and asks, 'Are you a *Peregrino*?' Shortly after, I am called to consult the doctor.

I try to explain in Spanish that my lower right leg and foot are swollen and discoloured, but she says, 'No. In English please. I worked for years in London.'

I tell her that a pharmacist diagnosed insect bites and ....'

'Diagnosed?' she interrupts, her status offended. 'Did he now? That's what I do.'

I submit to examination.

'Yes, these insect bites are infected... but you also have a problem with the circulation in that leg. You must have this checked when you get home. When is that?'

'In five days.'

Handing me a script for a more potent derma cream and antibiotics, she announces, 'The walk for you is over.'

'But would I be able to drive?' I ask. 'I'd like to explore the coast.'

'Maybe – in a couple of days.'

As I prepare to leave, she shakes her head and says, 'What are you doing over there? With Brexit.'

'Self-harm,' I say.

As I walk out, the tension over, the receptionist also asks if I'm okay. I thank him, and for Centro Médico.

I take the last (top-storey) box room in Pensión Suso, swallow my medicine and sleep. Until midnight, bass and drum pounds from the adjacent square as a prelude for a light show and fireworks.

Two days later, nausea receding and swelling reduced, I hire a car and begin to drive past scallop shell symbols on backpacks, on signs and in shop windows, reminding that all roads lead to Santiago, just as the grooves on the shell merge at a single focal point. Yet, sometimes, when things go wrong, the journey might lead you elsewhere – perhaps even to an island idyll eighty kilometres south.

CHAPTER 12

A Toxa's Study in Light

The Spiritual Variant hugs the shore of the Ría de Pontevedra at Combarro before climbing Mt Castrove to Armenteira and eventually emerge on the Ría de Arousa at Vilanova. But the coast between Combarro and Cambados holds more than one wonder.

Sunday afternoon brings my first sight of the Ría de Arousa – one of the many flooded river valleys that probe Galicia's coastline. Driving across the A Lanzada Isthmus I reach O Grove, and, on a whim, continue over a gleaming white, period bridge to the island of A Toxa. I park the car and wander ... past lavish houses, hanging gardens and spa hotels.

A glimpse of palm trees above purple bougainvillea draws me to an exquisite park, a haven for a unique treasure – a Romanesque Chapel, a study in light, gleaming like mother-of-pearl, covered in thousands of scallop shells.

People have gathered before its doors – some bowed down reading names and dates and prayers for healing, while others kneel, busily writing new entreaties over old.

A leaflet in the porch tells me this twelfth-century wonder is dedicated to the little-known San Caralampio and to the Virgen Del Carmen, patron saint of fishermen. I can't remember where I've already heard of Caralampio.

The Chapel of San Caralampio

The porch opens onto a simple nave and transept, a criss-cross vault and whitewashed walls inlaid with ships timbers. Fishermen would feel at home here, all its adornment outside.

Behind the altar, a figurine of the Virgin del San Carmen within a vertical shell, like a variant of Botticelli's 'The Birth of Venus' still rising from her scallop shell – but holding an infant Jesus. On her left, a statue of a bearded San Caralampio, arms outstretched.

Seated near the front, my eye is drawn to a stained glass St. James beside a Pre-Raphaelite St. Isabel. But this James seems far from otherworldly. His fierce face won't suffer fools gladly, reminding me of a conversation I once had with a Scottish Pilgrim under a similar window in Burgos.

'He's my kinda saint,' he confided. 'Nae pussy. Not gazing off into the middle distance as if he's about tae swoon.'

And he wasn't wrong. This James could easily portray a Calvinist Scot, as ready to swing a sword as a staff, a real 'Son of Thunder,' set to storm citadels or call down fire, his inner Presbyterian come to the fore.

This Chapel, now somehow bigger on the inside evokes a string of memories: of childhood summers on the Antrim Coast, rock-hopping along the shore or bike riding switchback roads, tracing out the curve of the bay to another profile, of Ballygally Head. Then stern, stoic Cairncastle Presbyterian church: the dignity of generations blazing from metrical psalters... *Ardens Sed Virens*: bushes burning but not consumed. A place in which this James might feel at home, among Ulster-Scots and Authorised Versions.

A 'Perdone señor,' brings me back to the present. I stand as grandparents and granddaughter take their seats until the church is almost full. As others stand, I prepare to leave but, suddenly, the priest appears. Trapped, I sit back down.

At the sharing of the peace, I'm struck by the smiles of this summer-happy congregation in their home space. As the liturgy is called out, they respond in chorus. I don't know the words, but the tune is familiar, if out of context.

It's Dylan's, 'Blowing in the Wind.'

And suddenly, emotion – that my journey should have unexpectedly brought me here, to this oasis off the pilgrim road.

How many roads indeed has it been? Trying to grasp the magic of these places, the breadcrumb trail of James and his Carpenter Messiah – the ones who set all this in motion, and still draw so many of us in their wake.

Afterwards everyone files out. But I go back in and just sit. Soon, others wander in. A couple kneels close to the front. The woman whispers something to him, rises, runs her hand across his back and leaves. He stays for some minutes, head bowed. Another couple take one another's photo in turn before la Virgen del Carmen and compare shots.

They come and go in ones and twos, treading softly, standing for moments in curious wonder before statues or stained glass, as if nostalgic for something they'd long lost. Or never had.

Perhaps *this* is another of T.S. Eliot's places where prayer has been valid – a place of intimacy and simplicity as against Santiago's grandeur.

I approach La Virgen del Carmen set within her scallop shell – a symbol of the Goddess Aphrodite (Venus) long before its appropriation by Jacobean pilgrimage. Aphrodite, shell-cradled, was blown ashore by the west wind, and became a symbol of love and fertility; her myth, woven through with all its strands of loss and heroic resurrection, even prefigures the Christian story.

Aphrodite fades, but San Carmen comes forward – virginal queen of heaven doubling as the queen of the sea, mother to those wresting a living from the ocean's chaos; a myth absorbing its own echoes, re-tasking for a new era, but with its purpose unchanged: delivering life lessons.

CHAPTER 13

San Caralampio – A Potential Pilgrim Patron

San Caralampio's statue attracts fewer admirers. He wears a golden chasuble (sleeveless vestment) symbol of the Resurrection, a palm branch in his right hand; in his eyes, an expression of suffering and compassion.

The leaflet tells me only that he was a priest and leader of the Ephesian Church, who refused to deny the faith and was executed on the orders of the Emperor Sauiro in 211 AD. Why then, is he remembered here?

I approach someone who comes to pin a notice in the porch and enquire in halting Spanish if there is any more information on the saint.

'Are you English? Are you a pilgrim?' he asks.

I say no, and yes, 'Soy irlandés,' and explain that I've just finished walking, and am now exploring.

He stands back from his notices, and states, 'You like our chapel.'

'Very much so.'

He points to San Caralampio, then chops his right hand into left. 'He suffered terrible torture.'

I assume dismemberment.

'But he wouldn't deny the faith. His dying prayer was that wherever he was remembered, the local people would be free from plague, enjoy the fresh air and have health in their bodies and souls. It is said that God granted his wishes.

'Yes,' he says nodding, 'he has special powers to heal diseases of the skin. That's why people come here from all over Spain, to our waters.'

Then looking over his spectacles, he raises an imaginary glass to his lips, tipples it back and forth, and adds, 'He is also the patron saint for ... drunks.'

My eyes widen.

'Yes. *And* the lame. A man I know comes here for one week each year. He can only walk a little but drinks a lot. He says there is peace, compassion in the saint's eyes. Even for such as him. Yes, every year. But not this one ... yet.'

I nod and think Caralampio a fitting patron for pilgrims, adept as we are at drinking, and limping, hobbling like zombies first thing in the morning. Might he have room in his portfolio for us? Could he spare the time? But then, for him, time wouldn't be an issue any longer. It would be a matter of inclination.

When I share these thoughts with my advisor, he leans his head to one side, and with the hint of a smile, says, 'I don't know. He's very busy now ... but in the quiet season, perhaps you could ask him then.'

He's fully occupied today, as busloads arrive and a flock of bangle sellers descend on the seekers of health and lost youth.

I take the advice proffered as I don't want to try the patience of a saint.

My friend has to leave, and unforgivably, I forget to ask his name, as I recalled where I'd heard of San Caralampio before, on the final stages of the Camino Francés. *He* was the saint emblazoned like a Pavarotti on the T-shirts of dozens of young people carrying industrial-sized containers of red wine – who had been worked into a bacchanalian frenzy by a samba band uniformed in orange T-shirts, blue kerchiefs, white trousers and porkpie hats. A Macarena shuffle; no 12 step programme ... Caralampio's martyrdom and elevation transformed into a sainted excuse for alcoholic abandon.

Outside, I walk into a healing breeze, a mistral wind from across the ría, and realise that the saint is the perfect patron for a spa retreat in O Salnés, this place of salt pans, saline springs.

A road takes me on a circuit of the island, past manicured lawns and lavish topiary, and into a wind soughed beech and pine forest leading to a donkey sanctuary and shell motifs set into paving.

But the church of San Caralampio is the pearl in this oyster. A sanctuary fit for calloused hands, a reminder that it was shepherds and fishermen, the ritually unclean, who were stable-called to witness new beginnings, or a Messiah's first miracles.

But, more prosaically, tonight I need a room.

CHAPTER 14

O Grove

Driving back across the bridge I find a small hotel run by another Carmen – this one a languages graduate.

My pack stowed, I return to the bar, order a drink and tell her I've just been to A Toxa and the Chapel of San Caralampio. 'That covering of shells. I've never seen anything like it before.'

'Yes,' she responds, 'it's special, but not just decorative. Many fishermen's houses were once covered in scallop shells – as protection against damp. They love that Chapel.

'You know of the legend of A Toxa?'

I shake my head.

'It was once a deserted island like Cortegada now – just past Villagarcía.'

'That's hard to believe. With all those hotels and apartments.'

'I know, but it really was. The legend is that a priest owned a donkey with skin problems but couldn't bring himself to kill it. So, he turned it loose on A Toxa at low tide. A few months later, a fisherman recognised the same donkey, full of life, enjoying itself rolling in seashore mud, it's skin completely cured.

'It was then they realised the waters were thermal, sulferal, hot water portals. And that the mud helped lung and skin conditions. So they built a bridge, a spa centre and hotels, even one for poorer people. From then on, it became a famous place of healing.'

'So that explains a donkey sanctuary,' I say.

'Yes, in memory of the legend.'

Later I read that the Romans also utilised the hot springs of A Toxa, so its healing properties can hardly have been a recent revelation, with O Salnés already famous for waters that regenerated skin and soothed aches. Yet this place of healing was supposedly forgotten for centuries – until the story of the donkey appears to gather in the folk memory of Ages when skin problems and plague were common, and which venerated any place that held out hope of healing.

Carmen tells me that the bridge was built in 1907. 'In the 1940s, Franco gave A Toxa to Countess Fenosa, a member of a rich industrial family, and most of the island was privatised. But we locals protested, and a central area of forest was retained for public use.

'The tourist office is still open if you want more information on O Grove. There is much to see.'

At the Tourist Office, Cecelia supplies me with maps and leaflets and urges me to visit the shellfish market, and even return for the famous seafood festival in October, which draws people from all over Spain.

I nod a perhaps.

'*Here*, and *here*,' she circles my map, 'is a boardwalk past the Piedras Negras. And *there*, an interesting Chapel at A Lanzada. But you must also visit Mount Siradella, 'where we hung the Meco.'

'The what?' I ask.

'No. A who.'

The Legend of the Meco

According to her story, a tradition existed that gave the Nobles a right to sleep with the bride-to-be of their subjects – the right of the first night. In French, the *droit de seigneur*.

In O Grove, as some priests were feudal overlords, the priest of Saint Martin demanded the same bridal right before he would conduct the marriage ceremony for a couple. He was called The Meco. He came from Madrid.

Eventually, the local people had enough and decided to kill him. So they brought him to Mount Siradella and hanged him from a fig tree. When the local magistrates came to investigate the killing of the Meco, the locals all claimed guilt, saying, '*I* killed the Meco.'

'A time when a predator priest met a #metoo Spartacus moment,' I suggest.

'Almost,' she suggests. 'But no one was convicted, and the magistrates and soldiers eventually withdrew. His effigy still hangs from a fig tree there.'

I ask when this had happened.

Her eyebrows raised, she reminds me that 'It's *a legend.*'

For a moment, I'd forgotten.

I'd been aware that Bishops were also feudal lords whose tyrannical abuses sparked the peasantry's *Irmandiños* revolts in the fifteenth century. The Meco then seemed the perfect archetype of clerical and feudal abuse, the personification of an evil system imposed by an outsider from that den of oppression and immorality, Madrid.

Language and Independence

That night, reading in the hotel's bar/restaurant, the television blares out news on the mounting crisis caused by Catalonia's independence vote.

Carmen directs a tirade at the screen. I'm unsure if the 'madness' she mentions refers to the protestors or the Government's over-reaction. And I wonder why the country's poorest, and, until recently, the most underdeveloped, region seems so content with its place in Spain.

So I pluck up courage to ask about the absence of an independence movement here, like in Catalonia, or the Basque country? I make the point that most Galicians seem happy to be Spanish, even though many speak Galego. And that a language movement usually produces a nationalist one also. 'It seems a mystery that it hasn't happened here.'

'You think so?' she says, her eyes rolling, her demeanour less accommodating than earlier.

I try again. 'I've heard it argued that the very idea of Spain was born in Galicia, which has the discovery of the tomb of St James at its heart. So, as Santiago, not Madrid, is its spiritual centre, why tear it away?'

'Really? Is that what *they* say?' she responds. 'No, no, no, it's much simpler than that. *I* will tell you the real reason Galicia is different from Catalonia.'

'*There*, the biggest party, the Nationalist Party (which is of the Right) is *for* independence, and the Socialists are against, while *here*, the Nationalist Party (the People's Party) is *against* independence. Only the Leftist Bloque Nationalista is pro-independence. They got the votes of my son and a few of his friends,' she laughs.

I refrain from mentioning that they actually got 8% of the vote, the PP nearly 50% and the Socialists (also anti-independence) almost 18%.

She goes on. 'Here, the population is much more conservative than Catalonia – and older, so they are more inclined to the Right. Many more of our young people still emigrate.'

'But what about the poorer working people?'

'Have you met any fishermen or farm labourers? They are the *most* right-wing. We have this cultural thing … about the value of hard work – a "just get on with it" mentality instilled from school days.'

Her eyes light up as she asserts: 'Anywhere in Spain, if a firm is starting up, they want *a Galician* on their team.'

'But what about the language?' I insist, and mention having read someone saying, 'If we are a nation, that is because of the language.' But now, I reason, with 80% speaking Galego, it's unusual to have different languages in a single state.

'So how do you explain Belgium or Switzerland? Or Wales?'

I can't.

Having won a victory, she softens her tone and contends that the language issue is exaggerated. 'If we want to move, to work, we need Spanish, English, or German. It's not all about speaking Galego.

'Anyway, the Galician language is very close to Portuguese – no matter what people say. It has a common root: we spoke the same tongue until the early Middle Ages.

'And the E.U. are not keen on any more breakaway states, thank you very much!'

She looks pointedly over her glasses, then continues.

'You should know that Galego is only spoken widely in small towns, where people learn it from their parents and grandparents.

Even then, dialects differ from place to place. Only a tiny minority speaks it exclusively.

'Most of the Galician speakers learnt it in school. They are what we call the *Neo-Falantes*, and what's taught is a mix of differing dialects. So much so that my mother, who only speaks Galego, said she can't understand Galician TV!'

We both laugh and she returns to her theme.

'The *Independiencia* people, like my son and his friends, are obsessed with the language. They live in a fantasy world. They think if we leave, the cows will give more milk, the mussels will jump into the pots and cook themselves, and all the women will love them more.'

She pauses for breath and reminds me that she has work to do. 'I'm closing the bar. Your tutorial is over.'

But she is unable to let the topic go. Clearing the dishes from a table, she says, 'Yes, there was a Castellan conquest, and we're just that little bit angry – but time moves on. We have the new normal – just like your UK, with England the dominant partner. But there is a British identity also, isn't there, over and above an English one?'

'But many in Scotland wanted to break away,' I say.

'But not the majority. Those for independence lost. Now all of you want to leave us and go your own way.'

'Not all of us.'

'Enough of you.'

She retreats into the kitchen for some minutes, and I'm left to reflect that perhaps Galicia is happy to imagine itself merely as a distinct, cultural community, yet part of a wider entity.

For most Galicians that is enough. What they want is respect – respect mainly granted via recognition as a Historic Nationality.

Why then run the economic risks of independence? Perhaps it's not such a mystery. Why would people inherently conservative not want to conserve the best of democratic-era Spain? Any anger they show against Castille seems false.

This is another example where constructive ambiguity can create a space in which two communities can imagine themselves part of different states. Only marching feet and mass rallies threaten instability. But here again, Galicia is not Catalonia.

Returning to dim the lights, she bids me Goodnight, and recommends that I should go up to Mount Siradella tomorrow and find the Meco's fig tree. 'We can be radical … but only sometimes!'

Mount Siradella – An Historic Viewpoint

Fresh-washed morning air. Tall trees. A winding carpet, a pine-needle path all the way to the lookout.

At the interpretive centre, a film explains that this place is part of the *Umia-O Grove Intertidal Complex*, with its unique variety of avian life, flora and fauna. Here rivers flowing into the Arousa estuary bring rich nutrients and fertile feeding for migrating birds or wintering refugees.

The film mentions so many species that I have to ask Greta, a German ornithologist, for more information. She gives me a leaflet in English, and, better still, walks with me to the lookout point above the centre.

She points East, to where 'The Bay,' stretches from the A Lanzada Isthmus to Cambados. Where the River Umia runs into lukewarm waters supporting over two hundred species in the dunes, wetlands and marshes, making it a haven for waders, oystercatchers, herons and egrets. I resolve to find out more about this Río.

At the shoreline, the distant, dark shapes of men and women, bent double, harvest cockles. Coaxing a living from the tide's rise and fall.

To the West is Bodeira Lake, a coastal lagoon where grebe and mallard breed alongside summer swifts.

While northwards, curlews and sandpipers needle the Illa de Arousa's shores. Greta's eyes shine as she stresses the importance of conserving such places that maintain migration movements and the survival of endangered species.

I tell her of the winter refuge for the brent geese at Strangford Lough in County Down. And how they bring hope to many, so beautifully captured by Mary Oliver's *Wild Geese* poem.

A party of schoolchildren arrive. She has to hurry back – but not before she gives directions to the location of the Meco's Fig Tree.

'You can't miss it,' she says with a wry smile. 'It's just off the track below, towards the remains of the Celtic Castro.'

There I find a figure fashioned somewhere between scarecrow and large doll swinging from a fig tree. Once home, I checked Father Martin Sarmiento's journals. He visited O Grove in 1745 and reports witnessing an annual parade in commemoration of these events, then being ushered to the gallows fig tree, and assured by excited locals that the figs are 'Red from the Meco's blood.' He dryly notes the red hue of the figs but suggests the cause lies with the height of Siradella and its cold winds rather than with a lynching.

Steep steps lead up to the remains of an Iron Age Celtic Castro.[13]

Somewhere nearby lay the legendary lost city of Lambriaca, its lands supposedly under the protective spell of a *river of oblivion*, which if crossed, wipes away the invader's memory of home. Averse as the Romans were to crossing rivers and seas, their arrival, in 137 BC, broke the spell.

Some have argued this area to be the site of the mythic Cassiterides Islands, with their valuable tin and lead mines. Roman writers Pliny and Strabo even located them off the northwest coast of Iberia, where the islands of Ons, Sálvora, and Ceis were laced with tin and lead, as well as harbouring dreams of eternal youth.

Apart from a view over sea-kissed A Toxa is a panorama of much of O Salnés – where *Salinas* (salt pans) shimmered in the heat. Its once bustling Celtic commerce (Phonecian franchised) ensured the preservation of fish and meat. Until the Romans launched a hostile takeover.

Then Christianity arrived, borne perhaps by a fisherman apostle. Yet the first church buildings date from the sixth century.

But some Pre-Roman Celtic traditions persist in the legends where nymphs, elves and fairies roam Siradella at dawn and dusk. While other mysterious beings (Mouros) like leprechauns manage to hoard treasures under abandoned Castros.

Viking raiders were attracted by this area's wealth where the rías similarity to fjords must have struck a chord, beckoning them to penetrate further inland.

But the discovery of St James's tomb in 813 A.D. drew eager Arab raiders and pirates to Santiago's pilgrim treasures.

Fortress castles, built to warn of approaching ships, became part of Santiago de Compostela's *Forward Defence*. A Lanzada, San

Sadurniño, Castelo de Lobeira, Cortegada and the Torres do Oeste at Catoira, became collectively known as *The Doors of Compostela*.

Mt Siradella, 'The Watcher' rock

I imagine eager eyes picking out Viking longboats, Arab dhows or pirate ships, then hastening to light warning beacons and rise smoke from pyre to pyre … all along the watchtowers as far as Padrón, where others leapt on fleet-footed horses, breathless for Santiago.

I descend and take a short stroll along a switchback boardwalk past the Piedras Negras (Black Rocks). And a lingering look to where Ons and Sálvora seem to float suspended above the waves.

CHAPTER 15

A Lanzada

Across the isthmus lies A Lanzada, and, by the Capilla de Nosa Señora, the excavated remains of another Castro settlement. The Capilla's simple, twelfth-century Romanesque structure, topped with terracotta tiles, was built on the remains of an older church linked to a tenth-century fortress. Today its only decoration a simple rose window, with the roof of its apse concave topped in the shape of a scallop shell.

The Capilla de Nosa Señora

Its dark and musty interior of thick stone and cool air houses a Baroque altarpiece, and a notice dryly describing feverish traditions.

Troubled by a curse from the Evil Eye? Starting from behind the altar, one should sweep the Chapel three times in a clockwise circuit.

A woman wishing to overcome infertility? Together with her partner, she must arrive on the last weekend of August and join a pilgrimage from Chapel to the breakwater beneath. Here, on a set of stones in the shape of a cradle, she allows herself to be bathed by nine waves. I double-take. *Nine waves.*

Here, where the beach faces west, where the death-rebirth ritual of the sun god descending into the ocean and rising again each morning has been witnessed by generations – a notice rather delicately urges the couple to 'earnestly desire' their much-sought fertility.[14]

The link to Celtic beliefs is clear. Their sacred number was three. Multiplied by itself and applied to waves, every ninth wave thus became a 'wave of transformation,' credited with extraordinary magical powers. Especially at the then world's edge, that hope would be magnified in a place fit for calling on gods and goddesses.[15]

The ritual of 'Nine Waves' appears in the eleventh-century Book of Invasions which outlines how the Gaels, or the Milesians, sailed from Galicia and arrived in Ireland.[16]

This origin myth tells how King Breogán, taken to be the founding father of the Galician Celtic nation, builds the city of Brigantia (forerunner to modern-day A Coruña) complete with a giant tower. (Other stories have Hercules as the labourer.)

From this tower, Breogán's descendant, Ith, a son of Miled, transfixed by the verdant beauty of the green land he spies faraway in the North-East, decides to sail there.

But after landing with a small party, he is ambushed and killed by Ireland's semi-divine God-Race, the *Tuatha De Daanan*, who fear invasion. Escaping home to Galicia, his compatriots swear vengeance. Sailing back, the Gaels' Druidic poet Amergin, a brother of the murdered Ith, comes with them.

Reaching Ireland, they travel inland to Tara, and confront the three kings who killed Ith. But these kings recognise wisdom in Amergin and offer to cede him authority as to how the issue is to be decided.

Amergin outlines the lawful mechanism for occupying land: to retreat a distance of 'nine blue waves' from the shore and wait on the open sea, a location belonging to the Gods.

'Then we will come back' he tells them, 'disembark and take the island by force. But if you can prevent us from setting foot on shore, we will turn our boats homewards and never trouble you again.'

Professor John Carey, of University College Cork, identifies this proposal as a ritual of arriving, of identification with place, rather than a 'land grab.'

The De Dannan Druids summon up a storm which threatens to destroy the Gaels. Amergin's brother, Don, focused only on conquest, wants to put all to the sword. But he appears to be judged, drowning in the storm-tossed waters.

Amergin calls out to the spirit of Ireland for help, praising its beauty. The storm ceases, and their boats are brought safely to shore – where he recites his epic poem:

> *I am the wind on the sea.*
> *I am the ocean wave.*
> *I am a powerful people.*
> *I am the eagle on the rock.*
> *I am the brightness of the sun.*
> *I am a fierce wild boar.*
> *I am a salmon in the pool.*
> *I am the wisdom of art.*
> *I am a sharp spear in battle.*
> *I am the God that puts fire in the brain.*
> *Who spreads light in the gatherings on the hill?*
> *Who can tell the ages of the Moon?*
> *Who can tell the place where the sun rests?*

They finally defeat the De Daanan, who like Siradella's *Mouros*, retreat underground, inhabiting the Neolithic tombs and barrows scattered throughout Ireland.

I sit on a bench and ponder these Celtic connections beyond Trega and Newgrange where another ritual has been re-enacted through the ages. A Lanzada seems to indicate that links between home and here may be more than mythic. In the Book of Invasions tale, the two lands seem to share a common language – or enough to facilitate communication. Both have their own Druids with a similar world view. Might these factors not indicate once active links, via trade in goods, ideas, stories, cosmology and myths?

New insights seem to suggest this possibility. Genetic research at Trinity College Dublin in 2009 suggested the closest relatives of the Irish may be in Galicia and the Basque Country. Though the 'may be,' must be stressed.

More tellingly, archeological evidence now shows that long before the supposed arrival of Celts in Ireland, circa 500 BC, peoples had been in contact for perhaps ten millennia. They sailed (the quickest means of travel) along the Atlantic sea lanes from Portugal, Iberia, to Gaul, Ireland, Scotland and the Orkneys.

These Atlantic-facing places were, as archeologist Barry Cunliffe and others posit, 'Zones of Connectivity,' almost a territory in their own right. And that this Atlantic *Fringe* or *Façade* (defined by proximity to the ocean) developed a shared cultural identity: these hard-working, hard-living, proud coastal peoples often had more in common with each other than their inland neighbours.[17]

The 'Celts from the West' thesis argues that what became the Celtic Languages of Irish, Breton and Gallic had their origins along this Atlantic Façade. Drawn from Phoenician roots, it developed into a Lingua Franca that enabled trade and the exchange of ideas.[18]

Tellingly, most surviving Celtic place names are located in the coastal regions. Therefore, Cunliffe and others posit that the *Celtic Fringe* is, in fact, the *Celtic Core*,' as where a culture originates is where its legacy lingers most.

According to this hypothesis, the Celtic Age may have spread first from West to East, long before the later migration from the East.

If this is correct, then Celtic identity is not ethnic, but *linguistic* and *cultural*. Its emphasis on a holistic worldview would resonate with, and be later absorbed within, an emerging Celtic Christian Spirituality.

* * *

Now I knew I must visit A Coruña, the supposed jumping off point for the Gaels journey.

SECTION 4
Seaways –
The First Celtic Camino

CHAPTER 16

A Coruña and a Tower
with a View

Seagulls cry above Santiago's Hospedería San Martín Pinario and, as a Hammer Dulcimer plays Magistera, I cast myself adrift on the swell of roads and let sea stories take me north – to A Coruña's Lighthouse – where I plan to take photographs of the place where a myth began.

All our seafaring tales draw, in part, from Ulysses' and Jason's Greek journeys. But Irish *Immrama* tales seem to seed later Galician ones.[19]

On the train, I read again of San Amaro, a tenth-century Abbot in A Coruña, who receives a command from God to build a boat and sail in the sun's path across the Atlantic to an earthly paradise.[20]

San Amaro finds this paradise housed in an enormous gemstone castle with rubied towers and battlements of gold. The gatekeeper refuses him entry but permits a tantalising keyhole glimpse of an eternal garden, where beautiful birdsong falls from Adam and Eve's Tree of Life, young musicians play strange instruments, and flower-crowned ladies circle in white.

Again refused entrance, he is informed that 300 years have passed since his arrival. He returns to the coast to find a city built and named after him.

Two centuries later, Trezonzonia, another Galician monk, likewise seems called to a paradise island. Climbing the tower of Hercules, he sees a heavenly land with a beautiful river. He sails to Ireland and settles by the Shannon which offers a view back to Brigantia's tower. After seven years, an angel commands him to return home. He refuses, contracts leprosy, repents, and returns.[21]

But, upon my arrival at the tourist information office beneath the lighthouse, a sinking feeling replaces excitement – as I realise I've lost my phone.

I explain to the receptionist that it's probably in the taxi I took from the estación. Unable to provide the driver's name or registration number, all I know is that it was a white taxi.

'They're all white,' she tells me.

Her thirty minutes of telephone calls achieve nothing.

Resigned to its loss, I walk to Breogán's statue and stare at his warrior shield and sword, beard and a shock of hair.

Breogán and the lighthouse

Then recall that he and his descendent Mil are generally believed to be the literary creations of Irish monks who placed them midst the Greek gift of a founding myth – a tower allegedly commissioned by Hercules, which was actually a Roman Lighthouse.

Iberian claims to be the Genesis of the Irish didn't appear until the Middle Ages, when Galicians took up the Breogán myth as *their* heritage, and with it the Irish as brothers.[22]

In 1602, Galicia's Governor, Count Caracena, pronounced Ireland 'the Spain of the North'. Some Galicians now say that that's why we are so sad. Because we took a wrong turn and got lost.

But if we did, we're making up for it in recent times in pilgrimage returns to Galicia.[23]

Beyond Breogán a vault of indigo sky, and atop the rock the tower rising fifty-five metres. The only Roman Lighthouse still in use, it's an eighteenth-century restoration with two-metre-thick walls around a second-century Roman core of chambers and a spiral ramp. The tower's wrap-around structure seems a fitting metaphor for myth wrapped around the monumental.

Its lantern once cast light from an enormous oil lamp onto a metal mirror. Projected out, the beam guided Imperial galleys to Brigantium's port, as oil, wine, leather, grain and salted fish were shipped back and forth.[24]

After the Romans left, a vibrant Atlantic trade system blossomed from the fifth to the eighth century. Working independently of the Mediterranean basin, ships carried grain, wine, oil, pottery, and ceramics from Bordeaux, north to Ireland, Scotland, Cornwall and Wales.

At a conference, I'd spoken to an expert on this era, José Sánchez Pardo of Santiago University. He believed such intense contact and trade along the Atlantic area engendered shared religious traditions.

'We have the story of the tenth-century boat, the Ui Chorra, bearing Irish monks to Northern Galicia,' he said. 'Plus, the striking similarity of the Suevic Parish List there to an Irish ecclesiastical one. It's unique in Spain.'[25]

It was during this period that the Irish monks took to recording earlier myths – another indication, he felt, of a simultaneous flow of ideas and literary transmissions between Galicia and Ireland.

Unlike elsewhere, they chose not to dismiss pagan beliefs as pernicious nonsense, but instead became reverent guardians of the past, recording and according respect to the old myths and legends – creating an allegory that tells a people who they are.

These Irish monastics had surely read Paulus Orosius, who, writing in 417 AD, remarked that maps of Ireland and Galicia seemed to be 'reaching out to each other.' He also talked of how the Brigantia lighthouse offered views as far as the Shannon.

Another author, Isidore of Seville, in his *Geographica*, (written in 636 AD) argued that the name Hibernia was derived from Hi-Iberia.

I asked how soon Ireland received copies of *Geographica*.

'Within thirty years of its creation,' was the reply. 'Surely a significant influence on the construction of the Book of Invasions.'

In academia it's termed a 'pseudo history', and, along with *Geographica*, its stories draw on traditional myths and folk tales originating in oral cultures.[26]

But perhaps it should also be known as *Mythic History*: the outcome of four centuries of Herculean labours by Irish Monks to place their ancestors in a biblical-style journey as if to a promised land; to give their people an origins story – a Mythos.

Joseph Campbell suggests that origin myths address the mystery and wonder of the universe, connecting us with the sacred realities of being. '*A myth is not a lie*,' he says, *Mythology is poetry, it is metaphorical*.'[27]

And there was a fund of folk tales and connections available on which to construct such a *Mythic History*, to relate peoples to their past, and find purpose and meaning there.

* * *

I muse on how Story and Myth reach out like hands in the darkness to touch-sense the face of what might be known though cannot be shown.

It seems clear to me that Amergin acts as a cypher for his authors' efforts to establish harmony with the past – long before a Chesterton or a Lewis argued that Christianity *fulfilled* paganism's search for The Divine, rather than replacing it.[28]

* * *

As I queue on the lighthouse ramp, I hear someone being asked if he was the Irishman who lost his phone?

My hand rises, relieved.

'A taxi driver rang and said he found it on his back seat. He'll leave it to the office later this afternoon when his shift is over.'

It seems that I've unintentionally organised something more than a snap-shot visit.

* * *

A staircase coils to where Ith once climbed to, on a winter's evening. I suppose he represents all who peered, as sailors do, beyond the known – pulled by some horizon event or pushed by a restless gene towards the restless ocean.

Like calls to like, with Atlantic peoples drawn out by a need to know; attracted to the apparent boundary where the sea meets not only sky but the elusively retreating Otherworld.

I stand where Ith gazed out, we are told, from a promontory (a sacred place for Neolithic and Celtic peoples) atop its tower that loomed large on minds and later maps, propelling him north, star-steered to his glimpse of green land.

On the rotunda below me, is a sky-blue mosaic dais which gives directions to places possessing a Celtic lingua franca: Kernow (Cornwall), Cymru (Wales), Mannin (Isle of Man), Alba (Scotland), Eire (Ireland), Galiza (Galicia), and Breizh (Brittany). Anglo and Saxon don't feature.[29]

I gaze out over the sea's swell, but a haze stretches across the horizon like a low white wall. I screw up my eyes, peer and peer but see only slivers of cloud snaking north like jet trails.

For millennia, the ocean was our means of connection until the Romans came and induced amnesia of the sea roads and the Atlantic community. Only now are we re-awakening to the fact that it was the sea that brought us together, not kept us apart.

Descending, I walk a circuit of the promontory – around a horseshoe bay, past rock and sculpted green, wildflower yellows and bubbling gorse, back to a bench at land's end before the same white wall.

It's in places like this, looking out over the ocean, that reveals something of what the poet Edward Thomas once sensed: 'The age of the earth, the greatness of time, space and nature, the littleness of man; the fact that the earth does not belong to man, but man to the earth'.[30]

A growing awareness rising again, earthed in a creed that Galician Celt and Druid also held to; one that burnished Patrick's Breastplate as he gathered to himself the powers of nature. A belief transmitted to Columba and Brendan – respecting the old tales, yet drawing them into a new one: the higher wisdom of *The King of all Things*. A tenet that created what Professor John Carey calls 'a hybrid, composite culture both wholly Irish and wholly Christian'.[31] A call that launched Peregrinati out in their hide boats to find desert places on the ocean. A practice blending a pre-Christian mythology of quest with the Christian desire to find an isle of paradise'.[32] One that coalesced in stories of the ever-elusive *Hy Braesil* in the far West, a metaphor of our longing for somewhere over the horizon; somewhere a place of peace for us.

It was how our minds once held together the paradox of being both matter *and* spirit. Though a place on a map really meant a place in the heart.

Eventually, awareness dawned that the paradise isle lay within and that *we* were 'the custodians', as the philosopher Heidegger held, 'of deep and ancient thresholds'.

CHAPTER 17

The Santiago Church by the Port

It's evening as I saunter the long walk back to the old port – busy now, busy since the Middle Ages when, according to records, it was quicker to sail to Santiago from Ireland or England than travel overland from León.

On 21st May 1456, 83 ships lay harboured here, part of a vast seaborne outpouring of pilgrims. Of these, 32 were from England and Ireland, others from Wales, Normandy, Brittany, even perhaps from the Baltic ports of Stockholm and Danzig.[33]

One of the ships that lowered its sail that day had on board the serial pilgrim chronicler William Wey, Priest and Fellow of the Royal College of Eton.

For the text of his sermon in the San Francisco church the next day he chose from 1st Samuel: 'Here I am. For you called me to this place.'

But my preference is for another place, the thirteenth-century Santiago church, right next door to the port, on the Rúa do Parrote. This the church that received so many Irish pilgrims fresh from disembarkation. Their first stop here for Mass and thanksgiving, and last stop on return voyages.

It also had a statue of St. James to embrace as warm-up for Santiago. It's now rarely open, but this Sunday evening I'm in luck.

Its ancient pulpit with a mermaid carved into its base has been moved to the side while James remains central in stained glass above and behind the altar, his halo spiked like a white circular saw.

But off high to the right, another stained glass figure catches my eye. This one has both a beard and turban, his eyes raised, his hands lifted, open-palmed. In question or worship? And to his left, a woman kneels, imploring.

I ask the verger '¿*Quién es?*' (Who are they?)

Of course. I should have known. They are Zebedee and Salome. Parents of St. James. Another holy family.

But I wonder if they were quite so smoothly reconciled?

After James' and John's lakeside call, their father Zebedee disappears from the Gospel narratives. Was he still angry about his sons abandoning the family business … for an unlicensed Rabbi?

Salome, though, seemed impressed by the Rabbi's claims, interceding with Jesus for positions of influence for her sons.

Here Zebedee seems reconciled, brushed onto glass and back into history.

I sit alone with them awhile, lulled by the silence of stone that has witnessed waves of pilgrims wash through this place, filled with expectation after landing safely from a long journey on their own quest.

Then a man enters, stops for a moment at the front of the church to appraise it, hands-on-hips. Seemingly unimpressed, he briefly continues his circuit and leaves, perhaps wondering what the fuss was all about.

* * *

The flight home climbs quickly over Galician forest and then vast green spaces between towns, village speckled. High over a city, I can make out factory funnels and a swathe of tenements tailing off to the coast, where I recognise the promontory and large tower, still monumental from ten thousand feet.

Then ships, their wakes trailing the sea all the way north as they have for millennia – perhaps even to a faraway green land with a Kerry coastline south of the Shannon.

To where I must also go.

CHAPTER 18

Waterville, Ballinskelligs Bay, Co. Kerry

'In this bay of memory, it was as if Amergin's words had sung themselves into bronze.'

Holger Lonze (Sculptor).

A boat's bronze prow rises from sun-drenched ground – a seafront memorial to the place in County Kerry where Celtic culture arrived long ago on the first day of May.

'It represents history breaking through,' Holger Lonze, its sculptor, explains. 'Its planking takes the shape of nine waves, in tribute not only to the Milesian Myth but to all the prehistoric sailors who voyaged past here without the aid of compass, charts or sextant; but relying only on wave patterns, solar and celestial navigation.'

The prow's tip has been designed to resemble a gannet's head, a large seabird with white plumage whose presence signals proximity to land; but this detail also alludes to the minor Skellig island that some days shimmers snow-white petalled.

Long before compass needles trembled over magnetite lodestones, our ship's course was guided by the bright North or Pole star, the only constant in the rotating heavens, then star clusters.

One appears in the sculptured gannet's eye, recalling the nymph Callisto's caution to Ulysses, in Homer's Odyssey, to take care on his sea borne return to Ithaca, to study the Pleiades cluster (the Seven Sisters) *and* the Big Dipper, whose rise in the early May sky signalled the sailing season.[34]

Amergin's boat breaking through

Holger's right to stress that location is important in mythology.

The authors of the *Book of Invasions* were certainly familiar with this place. Three of the 'takings' of Ireland happen around the Kenmare river and Ballinskelligs Bay (referred to in the text as Inverskena). And Kerry's bays, like Galicia's rías, also stretch far inland, suggesting association.

For this is mythic landscape: everything scaled up, writ large; a site fit for an origin drama in a natural amphitheatre.[35]

It's said that when Amergin, Druid and Bard, placed his right foot on the shore to recite his incantation, he brought to Ireland not only land claim but poetry. And not only to Ireland, as Robert Graves argued that, 'English poetic education should really begin not with *The Canterbury Tales*, not with *The Odyssey*, not even with *Genesis*, but with *The Song of Amergin*.'

Local poet, Paddy Bushe, is also here today as co-curator of the Amergin Poetry festival. He considers that the story of the Milesians fleeing war, drought and famine also gives the *Book of Invasions* text a renewed resonance in this era of mass migrations and climate change.[36]

He concedes that no historical evidence exists to back this Gaelic arrival story, though adds, paradoxically 'But the fact that it never happened doesn't mean it wasn't true.'

That's what *Sallustius*, the fourth-century Roman historian and mystic also thought. He famously wrote: 'Myths are things that never happened but always are'. Their nature allegorical. But behind the grandiose hidden truths and deeper insights lie that address questions of meaning and of the Divine. Again – *Mythic History*.

The thought occurs to me that perhaps even the Translatio Legend of St James's return to Galicia had also been influenced by *Immrama* stories such as St. Brendan's *Navagatio*. It was the very same Hand of God: '*Manu Domini Gubernante*,' that hovered over the Genesis waters of chaos; that piloted both Brendan across pages (in the ninth century) and James, later, in the twelfth-century *Codex Calixtinus*, the *Liber St Jacobi*.

I also wondered again if the string of ecclesiastical connections that Jamie Sanchez Prado had outlined to me could have led the Monks to look south for an origin myth?

* * *

Later Professor John Carey delivered a lecture on Amergin's Song, describing Waterville and Ballinskelligs as places saturated with its story.

Afterwards, I asked what was known about the poem's authors.

He shook his head. 'Very little. It's a mystery, much like the poem and its context.'

'Such a paradox,' I remark, 'Christian Monks effectively lauding a Druid and his pagan knowledge of sun, moon and tides.'

He points out that the monks were *also* supposed to know about such mysteries – and of how to mediate with the Divine. But they try to bring these mysteries within Christian belief, incorporating the past, respecting the two halves of Ireland's soul: the Gaels above ground, and the De Danaan below. 'There's a *balancing tension* here,' he states, 'of the unknowable, of mystery.'

Throughout the song *and* the Myth, he continues, emphasis is on the importance of balance and harmony between here and the Otherworld – 'which stands beyond the frontier of our mortal selves. And by insight, a flash of lightning or epiphany, we see the boundary.

'Amergin is the poet who awakes us to these places of the imagination. We could call it a meditation on being or a hymn of praise to the *divinity of the imagination.*'

* * *

As shadows lengthen, I wander the water's edge trying to picture unnamed monks – labouring down generations in scriptorium and cell, as Scribes, not Pharisees, their eyes strained, bent over vellum as candles gutter, blowing on cupped hands blued from ink and winter, gathering in the past with its various strands, braided together in an endeavour to trace Irish origins back, even unto a son of Noah.

For them, a new *Ninth Wave* had swept in, replacing capricious Gods, revealing the true face of the Divine as Love. The new *Way* presented as the first non-tribal religion, open to all; a new community of the imagination, leaving space for mystery, for wonder, (as in Celtic spirituality) allowing the De Daanan to become the soul of the land, restoring an Irish 'Eden Memory.'

Perhaps their explanatory template was also oriented to arrivals from the south and east, (because of monastic contacts *and* folk memories of Anatolian family migrations) rather than to the later, north-eastern, warrior-band Steppes invasions.[37]

And if the monks' purpose was to promote harmony and cap cycles of violence, might that not also help explain why they selected the South?

* * *

As the light leaches and the giant sun glows red, the wind slingshots swallows away, and I remember a sermon given in Harbour Faith Community in Carrickfergus, County Antrim. The Hebrew word for 'holy,' was *Quadosh* – something very different from notions of

84

personal piety; something much broader, encompassing notions of 'other', 'mystery' and 'wonder'. Birds in flight were such a wonder; a sunset was holy mystery; a newborn child Other, *Quadosh*. All were the opposite of '*Chol*' (sand) ordinary, mundane.

Most of our lives are sand, Pastor Steve Ames said.[38] But sometimes we get a glimpse of the transcendent, a moment of connection coming even through tales scribed with love in scriptorium and cell.

* * *

The Venerable Bede (c. 673–735) records in his *Ecclesiastical History of the English People*, his own received tale of *Quadosh*.

A council of elders were called by King Edwin of Northumbria to debate whether they should convert to Christianity.

One elegantly offered that 'The present life of man upon earth, O King, seems to me in comparison with that time which is unknown to us like the swift flight of a sparrow through the mead-hall where you sit at supper in winter with your Ealdormen and thanes, while the fire blazes in the midst and the hall is warmed, but the wintry storms of rain or snow are raging abroad. The sparrow, flying in at one door and immediately out at another, whilst he is within, is safe from the wintry tempest, but, after a short space of fair weather, he immediately vanishes out of your sight, passing from winter to winter again. So this life of man appears for a little while, but of what is to follow or what went before we know nothing at all. Therefore, if this new teaching has brought any more certain knowledge, it seems only right that we should follow it.'

Set against the immensity of the cosmos, Bede's humble sparrow appears here as a metaphor of our own brief, earthly journey from winter to winter, mystery to mystery.

I didn't know then that the places I'd revisit in the summer would reveal both more of their hidden histories *and* further connections.

Waterville's night boat

SECTION 5
On the Central Route

CHAPTER 19

Redondela

The Camino has its own irony. Often it leads us along laneways through a land torn by bitter conflict – our eyes so fixed on the remote past, or the goal of Santiago ahead, that we walk right through and miss the stories of places on the way. Like Redondela, where the coastal and central routes conjoin; where hidden histories simmer below the surface, alongside lessons on how to deal with the past.

It was October 2012 when I first encountered Redondela during a long day's hike from the hill village of Mos to Pontevedra. But this town seemed to hold something more than the sing-song syllables of its name as they rolled off the tongue.

Sometimes a place, like people, reveals itself only slowly.

Arriving here at midday five years later, I'd have time to explore. Finding a small room in a pensión just off the Plaza de Ribadavia, I wandered around Alameda Park, past the poplars, pines and planes that towered over benches set into privet hedges. Leaves tumbled over gravel gathering beneath late-season roses, yellow and red.

In the park's tourist office, I sign up for an evening walking tour, then sit to study the ornate period houses opposite, the cascading green of their balconies, blurred in the afternoon heat.

Five of us introduce ourselves at the start of the tour. We are made up of Maria, our guide, two American pilgrims, Jordi, from Barcelona, and me. Our eyes meet. The unspoken weight of Catalonia's latest crisis, its secession lessons – hang heavy in the air.

But Maria quickly ushers us into the safety of the remote past, telling us that a Roman Villa's remains found nearby may have given the town its name.

The town did indeed spring from imperial ambitions. The sandalled feet of Rome's legionnaires marched north along the Via Romana X1X, from Braga to Lugo, then east to Astorga – the point where mined gold and copper was collected. Later, in the Middle Ages, the Camino and the coast powered Redondela's development, the town becoming a major fishing port.

We wander through streets little changed since the fifteenth century, past the bespectacled statue of Alfonso Castelao, local artist and writer. At his feet are found representations of the dwarf fishermen of local legend – the town's founding fathers. Castelao, according to Maria, 'was famous for his many paintings of the little men who lived to eat and drink'. Close by she points to a few remaining fishermen's houses with their thick, white-washed walls and protruding corbels.

We saunter on to the fourteenth-century Casa da Torre, once part of the old town's walls, now recommissioned as an Albergue.

'That's where we're staying,' Jenny from Boston says. Yesterday she and her sister began their walk from Tui, preferring this quieter route to the final stretches of the Camino Francés. And they're not alone. After Sarria, Tui has become the most popular starting point as more of us hunger for how the Camino was twenty years ago.

Opposite the Casa stands a sixteenth-century manor house, the Pazo of Petán, a seat of power built by the Castilian Prego de Montaos family, their coat of arms – three towers and arches – appearing high on walls everywhere.

'The town hall,' Maria says, 'was built last century in imitation of the style of *these* manor houses.'

We look up at one of the two nineteenth-century railway viaducts that introduced modernity to the town. Then returning Argentinian emigres brought their plans for the construction of 'eclectic' and 'art nouveau' style housing, with large windows, ornate balconies, and courtyards full of magnolia trees.

'The early twentieth-century was a period of elegant modernisation,' Maria says, as we halt before another Pazo (a type of Galician manor house). 'The textile industrialist José Regojo renovated this one, finishing it off with a palatial flourish.'

Her brown eyes glow with fascination for this fragile era of eclectic aesthetic – a Galician Belle Epoque. A time twinned with the dreamy summers and refined tastes of Edwardian England before the *Guns of August* swept an Age away, just as Spanish arms did 22 years later, in July, 1936.

Her reverie over, her tone suddenly changes, as she stresses that Regojo's Redondela-born wife, Rita Otero, was famous for her good works for the poor and the orphaned. 'In 2015, we renamed this street in her honour.'

Our tour closes before a large black-and-white photograph on a gable wall, with Maria asking, 'Do you recognise this place?'

We crowd round and peer intently at a portrait of a quay, its fishing boats emblazoned with the names of sweethearts, gods and goddesses. Over the bow of one sits a teenage boy in a white shirt and slicked-back hair, dangling his legs as a besuited man strolls past young plane trees fronting familiar houses, layered onto a hill.

'Is that … how the main street once looked?' Jordi from Barcelona asks.

Maria beams, clapping her hands at his answer. 'Yes, yes, it's the Rúa Ribeira. In the 1920s, the river was channelled to access the ría directly so that the harbour fell into disuse. In the 1960s it was filled in, to create Alameda Park, and the bandstand added – in the older style.'

Maria has unpacked for us the town's layered Ages: from Roman occupation to seaport, from pilgrim halt to feudal garrison and from elegance to industry, its competing *Golden Ages* seeming to merge effortlessly each into the next: the town hall reminiscent of older Manor Houses, and the harbour filled in and furnished with a bandstand to evoke a period feel. Imitation games that cherished continuity. But I wondered what other stories might lie hidden behind Redondela's facades?

Chapter 20

A Sister and Brother –
Rita and Alejandro Otero

Back in my room, and after I got home, I searched online for information on what provoked the philanthropy of Rita Otero and made her tithe her life to the poor?

Born in 1902, she met her future husband, José Regojo, at a business conference in Lisbon in the early 1920s, accompanied by her older brother Alejandro, a medical Doctor, Professor, and later deputy of Spain's socialist party, PSOE. Her marriage brought a textile empire to the town, and contrasting fortunes for brothers-in-law Alejandro and José.

At the outbreak of Civil War in 1936, Regojo Industries secured the contract to supply uniforms, shirts, breeches, boots and belts to Franco's army – while Alejandro Otero's politics forced him to flee Galicia.

The war over, Alejandro, now Vice-President of the PSOE and member of the Republican Government in Exile, was sentenced in absentia to 15 years in exile and a one million pesetas fine for crimes of espionage and rebellion. That night, an angry mob rallied in torchlight and stoned his abandoned home.

Meanwhile Regojo industries flourished, in its heyday employing 6,000 workers who produced a million shirts a year and perhaps ten million Salvador Dalí signature shirts.

In 1940, Alejandro sailed from Paris to Mexico where he worked as a medic with organisations committed to helping Spanish refugees and local people. Nuns who ran a clinic under his guidance wrote asking the Spanish Government if he might be pardoned because of his good works – but to no avail. His sister and he never met again and he died an exile in 1953.

The newspapers, however, make no mention of any of this, for here, the relationship with the past remains sensitive and complicated. I wonder at Rita's resilience in surviving this trauma of divided loyalties and loss.

I cease my note-taking, and walk back to her Pazo, imagining the grand parties once held in its palatial surroundings, the conspicuous consumption, the business favours asked and received – the choosing of sides. But tonight the house is silent; the chink of glasses occurring elsewhere in the streets and cafes and bars as pilgrims unwind. In the fading light I weave my way back through the revellers to read more of Rita.

Almost fifty years had to pass after Rita's death before Redondela publicly recalled her story in 2015. Then the local newspapers report a street-naming ceremony inner honour, as *Gaitas* played for her children, grandchildren, and civic dignitaries. In a video, her son testifies that she was a good woman 'with a heart in which everyone could fit'.

In an impossible situation, Rita seems to have drawn enormous strength from her faith; for rather than retreat from the world, she turned her attention outwards, 'never thinking of herself, always about others,' her son Pedro explains. Crediting her with 'an iron will,' he lists her values as: 'hard work, courage and compassion – with the doors of our house open to everyone, especially the poor. As a devout Catholic, she not only wrote to the prisoners on the island of San Simón but visited them, bringing clothes, food, and most importantly, love.'

Pedro's mention of San Simón alluded to one of a Gulag of camps for Republican political prisoners, to whom, with great courage, she showed compassion when it was in scarce supply. Perhaps she saw her beloved brother in their eyes, for, had he not fled, he would have suffered a similar fate.

Or perhaps she took to heart the words of the Carpenter Messiah of Matthew's Gospel: 'I was hungry, and you fed me; in prison and you visited me'. In a life worthy of imitation, her grandson acknowledged her 'spiritual legacy' and a 'social vision' which he hoped to pass on to his own children.

I put away my notes and tried to sleep midst the raucous revels spilling through the streets outside. And in the morning, I walked on, over the switchback path to Arcade and through a forest of eucalyptus, grateful that Redondcla had revealed more of itself.

CHAPTER 21

The Island of San Simón

Two years later, in July 2019, as I walked again from Porto, accompanied by fellow Camino enthusiast Brendan McManus from home, fate conspired to complete the story.

Arriving late in the afternoon, we can't find accommodation. All the tourist officer can offer is a room in a beach-front Pensión three kilometres further on, in Cesantes. I tell him of my previous visit, of my interest in the Oteros, and how, in dangerous times, Rita brought food and clothing to the prisoners of San Simón. 'But I didn't find out where it was,' I admit.

His eyes widen, and he turns and points to a large aerial photograph behind him of an island, its trees bubbling vivid green against the ría's blue.

'That's it,' he says. 'It's out in the bay just across from where you will be staying.'

An hour later, we stand on the Cesantes shoreline at high tide, looking out to San Simón and a smaller island next to it, with a bridge in between as if to clamp them together. Our efforts to hire a boat meet with no success, offline and on.

Then, later that evening, a phone number from a restaurant owner shifts all the gears, opens doors: for a lift in the morning back to Redondela, then to Vigo, and tickets for a tour boat to San Simón – with an English-speaking guide and a train back in the afternoon.

The Island of San Simon and a glimpse of the Rande Bridge

Our packed tour boat sets off into Vigo Bay and soon reaches the giant cabled Rande Bridge which straddles the ría and takes its name from the Battle of Rande which. in 1702, was part of an Anglo-French tussle for control over Spain, Lucia, our guide, explains. A fleet of Spanish galleons laden with gold and silver from the Americas was attacked by the English and to prevent the treasure falling into their hands, the boats were burnt, then scuttled.

'This scene was re-created by Jules Verne in *Twenty Thousand Leagues Under The Sea*,' Lucia points out.

Back home, I read how, shimmering under the lights of the *Nautilus*, Captain Nemo shows Professor Arronax the site where the galleons 'freighted for the Spanish Government had sunk. And here Captain Nemo came at his convenience to pack away those millions on his Nautilus. From cases and barrels tumbled ingots of gold and silver, cascades of jewels, the sand heaped with them'.

Even though Verne played into the legend of lost treasure at the bottom of Vigo Bay, in reality much of it had already been unloaded before the attack. His anti-hero alludes to Odysseus identifying himself to the cyclops as Nemo, 'nobody,' as both the captain and the Greek hero wander the seas in exile.

Lucia points across to Meriende's Fabrica do Alemán (Factory of the Germans), and explains its links to more recent conflicts. Once owned during the Second World War by the Nazi entrepreneur, Otto Gerdtzen Boye, it processed metals such as tungsten for German munitions, as part re-payment for their assistance in the Civil War.

It's now reverted to something more mundane – canning fish.

Docking ten minutes later, we file onto an island which has been repeatedly invaded, settled or sacked since it was first inhabited in the Bronze Age.

Here Vikings, Normans, and Muslims contested control of the ría, until, in 897, the first pilgrims arrived en route to Santiago, bringing Benedictines and Templars in their wake. The larger island was named after St Peter, and the smaller, San Antón, after Desert Father, St Anthony.

Francis Drake (to the English an Elizabethan buccaneer, but to the Spanish, a pirate) also plied his trade here, sacking the island, lopping off the hands of St. Peter's statue in the sixteenth-century church ... presumably to remove his hold on the Keys to the Kingdom.

In the nineteenth-century, as European trips became fashionable, transatlantic ships began to arrive from Spain's Latin American colonies and from the Philippines. But they also brought with them the danger of infectious diseases: cholera, TB, typhoid and smallpox. However, the islands' isolation provided perfect quarantine: San Simón, for standard checks, and San Antón, for those infected. The twin sets of gates on the bridge between allowed food to be put through at one place and collected from the other.

From 1838, San Simón was re-tasked as an almost Ellis Island, with differing accommodation for differing pocket depths. However, as new medicines and vaccines were developed, the need for quarantine lessened, and in 1927 the centre was closed.

Plans for its use as a spa were halted by the outbreak of the Civil War – the place now repurposed as a Prison Island, an Alcatraz equivalent, where the strong surrounding currents also discouraged escape. But a prison island became a Concentration Camp tasked to cleanse what was portrayed as ideological rather than medical infections from defeated Republican soldiers – and civilians with suspect sympathies.

Illness and disease returned once again to San Simón, but this time induced by cruelty, starvation, beatings and fear.

'Between 5,000 and 6,000 prisoners were held here,' Lucia tells me. 'About 1,500 at a time.'

The slave ship conditions included sleeping face to back in piles (set spaces) of no more than thirty centimetres wide, under constant guard, with no communication permitted.

Its first Director, Fernando Lago, became known as 'The Butcher of San Simón.' The second, Father Nieto, a Jesuit from Vigo, more religious but equally brutal, introduced a new Inquisition, of forced confession and obligatory attendance at daily Mass, which he celebrated with a pistol in his belt. This he drew more than once to administer 'mercy killings' to the wounded and ill via a single shot through the head.

I ask Lucia if many of the prisoners had been executed on the island and then buried in the ría.

'No, not many.' Usually it was, she said, via groups of ten or so, told they were being moved to Pontevedra prison, and then taken out for a *Paseo*, a walk there. On the way, they were shot by the side of the road and buried in the forest in unmarked graves ... 'along where the Camino goes,' she added.

I tail off from the tour in an effort to escape its unremitting bleakness – leaving behind the staged photos to make it look like a Holiday Camp, cloaking the truth of a ghost island of broken spirits, caged in a place of no return. Along with others throughout Europe.

In 1943, when it became obvious that the Nazis would lose the war, the island was evacuated, the prisoners spread throughout the region – the evidence removed, the stories denied.

That's how they came to terms with what was done. If you were a guard, you'd avoid, deny, and draw a veil over all; say that was in the past. But once denial stopped working, you'd attempt to shift the blame onto the victims, saying, '*We* carry the burden of what had to be done. Or 'look what they made us do.' In other words, 'We are victims too.' If further pressed, you might demand a one-sided *Pact of Forgetting*, insist the victims move on, leaving thousands of unmarked graves, the calling cards of the war criminal.

CHAPTER 22

What We Choose to Remember –
or Forget

After the Second World War, San Simón became an orphanage, officially for children of fishermen who went to school in Redondela and returned in the evenings. But after the Civil War, orphanages appeared everywhere in Spain as Franco created so many orphans… children of the Republican 'contagion' in need of harsh Catholic re-education.

This lasted until the 1980s when cries rose to a crescendo for the 'Recovery of Historical Memory'.

Redondela's Council responded by asking local artists to create statues for the island that would speak to the past. One of these, simply named 'Fear', set on the site of the orphanage, depicts a wide-eyed, terror-stricken boy – alluding to another generation of as yet untold stories, for San Simón remained a place of fear.

Another statue in the cemetery is of Ulysses, surrounded by the claws of skeletal death and despair.

Meeting with Achilles, when he later descends to the Underworld, Ulysses is told that fame is worthless compared to life. His task, therefore, is to survive hell and make it home. In San Simon, few were as fortunate.

On my way back to the dock, I see the final statue, of San Ero of Armenteira (on the Spiritual Variant), a robin on his shoulder, transported from forest birdsong bliss, his face now contorted in an almost Edvard Munch '*Scream*'.

Meeting up with Lucia again, I shake my head and say, 'This place…'

She nods and says, 'The first time I was here, it made my skin crawl, the hairs on the back of my neck stand up.'

We all could feel the malign Psychogeography rising like shudders of heat. From men who darkly despoiled the setting's beauty.

Brendan has been to Auschwitz. 'The feeling is the same – the spirits of tortured souls … clinging to this place still. There's little birdsong here either.'

Yet there *is* music, from *Gaitas* (Galician Bagpipes), played by young musicians on a weekend of Traditional Tuition. The island, full of boxwood trees from which their pipes are carved, now hears new songs: of both joy *and* lament – for no healing flows from denial.

The place, now repurposed as a centre devoted to all the Arts – poetry, prose, music, drama, sculpture and song – refutes and reverses Adorno's maxim that 'There can be no poetry after Auschwitz' – its activities offering a healing compress for the wounds of the past.

We cast off. The island recedes.

But its aura accompanies us as if net-caught and brought to shore – in order that we might speak out its stories.

Alfonso Castelao

I say to Lucia, 'This is such a credit to Redondela – ensuring the names of those lost in a time of terror.' I mention also how Rita Otero has been honoured.

'But all sides have been remembered,' she says. 'There's a Regojo street, an Alejandro Plaza and a statue to Alfonso Castelao.'

I tell her that I saw Castelao's statue, but he was described as an artist/caricaturist.

'No, he was much more than that. Look at the statue again more closely. He was a Galician Nationalist, then a member of both the PSOE (Socialist Party) and the Republican Government in exile.'

'Like Alejandro Otero,' I say.

'Yes, like Alejandro. Both of them doctors. And both died in exile.'

On the train back to Redondela I read more about Castelao, then walk to Alameda Park and study his statue. Cast in bronze in 1986, the centenary of his birth, it shows him dapper in a bow tie and large horn-rimmed glasses. Left foot forward, he clutches a book to his chest, its cover inscribed with the words, 'Thinking of Galiza' – a reference to his key work, '*Sempre en Galiza*' (Always in Galicia) – written in later life.

Not just an artist-caricaturist then, but doctor, politician and writer – his life dedicated to the promotion of Galician cultural identity. Writing nearly always in Galego, he asserted that, 'If we are a nation, that is because of the language' – as if nationhood can be spoken or written into being.

But he was both a nationalist *and* internationalist, visioning a Galician State in federation with other Iberian nations in a United States of Europe. His ideas, constantly evolving, oscillated from greater autonomy to federalism or secession, seeking to accommodate, 'our *relative values* with the *relative values* of the rest of Hespaña and the world'.

Then further connections with Ireland emerge. He also, along with Alejandro Otero, was forced to flee in the first months of the Civil War, first to Barcelona, then Paris. Here he wrote a letter of appeal from the Government in Exile to the people of Ireland – from where General O'Duffy's Blueshirts had been dispatched to fight on Franco's side. In his letter, he appealed to Ireland to support the Republic rather than aid the oppression of 'Your brothers in Spain'.[39]

Though Castelao's appeal was unsuccessful, the Blueshirts were later sent home after they engaged in a firefight with fellow Francoist forces – their only action. The *Generalissimo* noting wryly that 'when they were not drunk, they were at Mass'.

After the war, Castelao deployed pen and paintbrush to condemn the Nationalist regime. In life, he, along with Alejandro Otero, would never return. He died of lung cancer in 1950, in Buenos Aires, aged 64, seemingly forgotten, his dreams turned to ashes, to dust.

Then *hope and history rhymed* when Franco died in 1975 and in the ensuing 1978 New Constitution. This granted greater regional autonomy and recognised Galego as a 'Historic Language'. Heroes were borne home on journeys of delayed appreciation, with Castelao's remains re-interred in Santiago's 'Pantheon of Illustrious Galicians' in 1984. His and other stories were reclaimed and incorporated into the national one.

The Israeli academic Jacob Talmon wrote that 'The essence of tragedy is right versus right' and that in a tragic struggle, 'the victors become the guilty and must make amends to the losers'.

The enduring tragedy, historian and economist RH Tawney rightly notes, 'is that the discovery of the reconciling formula is always left to future generations, in which passions have cooled into curiosity, and the agonies of people have become the exercise in the schools'.

However, I like the scholar Ernest Renan's espousal of possibility, that a place, as well as a nation, can be defined both by what it chooses to remember, as much as by what it chooses to forget. And Redondela chose remembrance; expressed in street namings for Regogo and Otero: one for the accumulation of wealth, the other for its dispersal. Or the Plaza for Alejandro Otero in 2013. Or the statue in the park for Castelao. Honouring those once swept away by history.

I study again the photographs of Conservative and Socialist councillors, Peoples Party and PSOE, as they stand together at street-naming ceremonies, recognising the humanity of the other, learning from history lest it be repeated.

On a tree above me, a nightingale sings, its song falling like manna on a town once shaken to its core by political earthquakes. Now settled again.

Climbing out of the town, I look back on the ría and the Rande Bridge, its stanchions rising bright in the sun, its cables, sparkling silver, strung taut like a harp. And I'm grateful for having learned more of Redondela's agony and healing. Grateful also to have found twentieth-century saints, scholars and doctors – not sequestered in cloister walks but caught in tragic circumstances, mired in the mess of things. And that *their* stories have now become part of this land's no longer hidden history.

Section 6
On the Spiritual Variant

Then I found other mythic connections, not from the distant past but from the early Middle Ages.

CHAPTER 23

The Stone and the Story – Armenteira and Nendrum

An early morning climb through Mount Castrove's thick pine and eucalyptus. It must be close now.

A series of declining turns. A meandering stream. Until the path petered out onto treacly tarmac ... and my first glimpse of Armenteira's Monastery's bell tower – drifting in the swell of forest waves, rising, falling. I didn't know, on that 30th August, that I'd be back in all weathers, mist, rain and toe-damp cold.

I walked into the monastery's courtyard and learned from leaflets in its tourist office that the Cistercian order had an outpost here from the twelfth to the nineteenth century. But with secularisation of church property it declined into ruin.

Until 1963. The year a son arrived in search of the place that inspired his father, Ramón María del Valle-Inclán, to write, 'Aromas de Leyenda' (Aromas of Legend) poems inspired by Galician landscape, tales and traditions.[40]

Ramón's son Carlos Valle-Inclán went on to found the 'Amigos de Armenteira' who were dedicated to the monastery's restoration.

Twenty-six years later, its restoration complete, a call went out to the Cistercian sisters of the Monastery of Alloz in Navarre (between

Estella and Puente La Reina on the Camino Frances) to continue the story.

Under its cloister's intricate vaulting I read the Monastery's origin myth. It begins with Don Ero of Armenteira, his wife, and their unanswered prayers for children. Eventually, a revelation came, promising, instead, spiritual descendants. Ero later founds the Santa María Monastery, becoming Abbot, with 30th August his feast day.

His prayer then became petition for a taste of what heavenly bliss might feel like. One day, as he walked through the forest, he was struck by the lyric beauty of a bird's song. As he sat entranced for what seemed like mere minutes, he experienced an epiphany that brought him deep peace and contentment …

But this story I knew. And what would come next, echoing Mo-Choi's sojourn out of time, where eternal pierces temporal in Nendrum's origin myth.

As twilight fell, Ero walked back to the monastery, knocked on the door, but was greeted by an unknown monk who appeared not to recognise him. Asked to identify himself, he answers, 'I am your Abbot, Ero.' The startled monk calls others, who explain that Abbot Ero disappeared into the mountains three hundred years ago.

Then Ero realised that his wish to experience heavenly bliss had been granted, with three hundred years of deep contentment equating to mere minutes of birdsong.

As Nendrum dates from the early seventh century (500 years before Armenteira's founding), it seems Mo-Choi's tale set midst Irish forest birdsong, provided such a pleasing metaphor that it got franchised out and dispersed throughout the European-wide-web of Cistercian monasteries – sent south, to be cut and pasted in Galicia, with only names and places altered.

Then the source of the story began to fade with the arrival of the Normans in eleventh century County Down, bringing the Cistercian order in tow, to establish a rival monastery across the lough at Greyabbey. Its expansion and patronage soon led to Nendrum's decline.

But the tale seems to have taken wings and travelled even before the eleventh-century.[41]

These themes of slipping out of linear time, these shared sacred stories of miraculous monastic origins seem freighted also with Greek as well as Irish echoes. The myth of Tiresias tells of how he stumbled upon Athena bathing naked and was punished with blindness. The goddess later partially recants and releases two snakes that clean out Tiresias's ears, heightening his spiritual senses and enabling him to understand prophetic birdsong. The gift of Augery equipped Tiresias to then mediate between man and gods, present and future, this and the Otherworld.

Irish *Immrama* (Sea Voyager) questing tales, are similarly steeped in notions of stepping out of time. One famous example is 'The Voyage of Bran'. Eager to 'get away from the noise' of a festival, Bran walks outside and hears the beautiful music of the Sidhe, the inhabitants of the Otherworld. An ageless figure appears and sings, urging Bran to voyage across the sea to a land of beauty. He recruits companions and sails to an island of joy, living there for a year. Back home he is informed that Bran left hundreds of years earlier to seek a mystical land and has not been heard of since. Like Mo-Choi, St Virília, and now San Ero, Bran had slipped out of temporal and into eternal time.

I rose from my cloister seat and walked outside, to little activity: an occasional car or a few slow-stepped visitors making their way through thick heat. San Ero's Memorial Day passing almost unnoticed, slipped from memory just as he once slipped out of time.

* * *

Three years later I'm slow-walking Ero's forest once again, deep-breathing the scent of wind-stirred eucalyptus leaves, their glint like shoals of silverfish floating; like Nendrum's ash hangars, seemingly lit from within.

I'm overtaken by Brendan from home, and Sandro, Rita and Silvia from Italy, to walk into Armenteira together.

This is the fifth time in these three years I've been here – but its fascination endures: the wonder of stepping from forest to bell-tower midst a swell of green continues. Where nuns arrived from Navarre thirty years ago, to sing out The Hours again.

Atop the monastery's entrance arch – San Ero kneels before an avian enchantment, beside Madonna and Child

I touch the lintels of the courtyard's entrance: seven hundred years of memories sealed in stone, its story echoing home. Sister Áurea stands in the shop midst scented candles; she's frailer now, her right elbow supported by a crutch. I'd learnt on a previous visit that as Abbess in their Mother House, she had been the driving force behind the move from Navarre. Then she resigned her office as Abbess and came here as a cook. But on the sudden death of the first Mother Superior, she was again elected to the post, serving for a further ten years.

When she is joined by Catherine, a younger nun, I ask if we might meet later; I am keen to hear a little more about their community. I ask Brendan, who speaks fluent Spanish, to act as interpreter.

At six p.m. we are ushered into the quiet of a first-floor room, away from the hum of voices in the cafe-bar. I ask what Armenteira was like thirty years ago, and what had drawn them here.

'There was no electricity when we arrived,' Áurea says, 'No television, and even the bars were thinking of leaving. But the restored monastery seemed perfect. It was the stone and the story that drew us, plus the simplicity of the place and the people. The locals once lived by working stone, hence the stone statues in the church.'

She tells me that only eight sisters remain. The one who is ninety-eight comes down from her room only on Sundays.

I ask what occupations they formerly had. Catherine counts off on her fingers: 'Two nurses, three teachers, a psychologist, a forest engineer – and a fire-fighter. That was me.'

I think that her fire-fighting skills might yet be needed, given the outbreaks on Mount Castrove in 2017 which even threatened Vigo's suburbs.

'But now,' Catherine continues, 'our lives are defined by the Benedictine Rule, the spirituality of Saint Bernard, and a common practice known as *Santa Simplicitas* (Sacred Simplicity). It's reflected in our vestments, our rhythm of life, our food (mostly vegetarian, from the garden) and in the liturgy of The Hours.

'All these practices help me to trust in Christ and understand my own divinity.'

'Your own divinity?' I question, and Catherine turns to Áurea who nods, then uses the metaphor of a copy and its original to explain.

'Wrong paths taken can damage the likeness of Christ in us, but they never negate his image.'

Reaching across, her hand almost touching mine, she stresses, 'Marvellous things happen when you connect with the mystery inside.'

I tell her that that is not dissimilar to what I've learnt of Celtic Spirituality, adding that it's a far cry from the Augustinian model with its stress on our sinful, fallen state. 'It sounds more like Theosis, affirming the divine spark in all that only needs fanned into flame ... an emphasis on our wounded-ness rather than fallen-ness.'

She looks over her glasses and says, 'Fallenness is not a good starting point to get to somewhere better. But His image, stamped at our core, gives us hope.'

I tell them I've been reading something like this in Thomas Merton's work, with his notion of *Le Point Verge*.

Catherine beams. 'I love Thomas Merton. Yes, Le Pointe Verge, the point of pure nothingness inside, where we merge with God.'

I mention that in one of his last journeys, Merton stayed with the Cistercian sisters of Mount Redwood, in California.

'Yes, the giant redwoods fascinated him,' Catherine says. 'We too have a Sequoia forest, just above Poio monastery.'

'But Merton and the Mount Redwood sisters lived in utter isolation – to pray, contemplate, pursue their vocation.'

They nod, but don't respond to the cue. I hesitate, reluctant to trespass on the sacred ground of their calling, but still do.

'There's a real paradox here, isn't there?' I say. 'You chose this mountaintop place and forest isolation to live out your vocation. Yet the world has come afresh to you, with the Variante wending its way past your front door. That must create tension.'

They exchange quick glances. Then Catherine, head inclined, says, 'Under the Benedictine rule, the religious life has a certain rhythm to it – like a river. You drop down, submerge yourself in its flow and let it carry you. For us, prayer is not just part of the work, it *is* the work.

'But … we also need to read the signs of the kingdom; discern what is being asked of us. Our original intention wasn't to serve along a Camino, but the Camino has come to us – an obvious sign.'

She looks round the room a moment, then continues: 'We are not a hostel, but we offer hospitality. We'd like to be able to offer one-to-one prayer and support – something like Santiago's Camino Companions, but there are too few of us. We do what we can.'

Áurea adds: 'Part of our work now is to bring a sense of peace and blessing to the pilgrims each evening, which can be very meaningful for them.'

The clock on the wall strikes six-thirty, summoning them to preparation for Vespers at seven.

We thank them and walk to the hum of bees among their courtyard Camellia trees, as I marvel at the soft power of these lives lived in service.

A covey of pilgrims and day-trippers cluster expectantly around courtyard and cafe-bar tables. I'd assumed, wrongly, that the Variante route was responsible for reinvigorating this place. But its rebirth began long before – with the arrival of the sisters and a tourist office that sensed a story to promote, hoping that visitors would overflow into Albariño festivals and bodegas throughout O Salnés. And people came. For even as monastic communities retreat, their practice of prayer and silent contemplation, seems to draw others like an invisible force as if to a still-point in a spinning world.

Vespers

The organist sets her stops to descant. The nuns and Santí (a Cistercian monk from Sangüesa) file in and sit in a semicircle facing the altar. Late arrivals with backpacks trickle in, fresh from the track. Perhaps twenty of us are here as we listen to the pilgrim blessing spoken in Spanish, Portuguese, French, Italian and English.

The invocation, 'May all your roads rise to meet you and carry you safely into the arms of Santiago,' recalls the 'Irish Blessing' – for a journey on foot, walking downhill, the wind at your back, sun on your face.

I look across to see Rita's eyes welling up as she mourns the loss of a lifelong friend, and I swallow hard as we are invited forward. Some stand awkwardly, shuffling into another semicircle, bemused eyes scanning left and right, wondering what will happen.

A mother beckons her young son forward, drapes her arms over his shoulders and pulls him close. As the nuns sing a simple Taize chant, Santí gently places his hands on each forehead, and offers a silent prayer.

As he reaches me, something happens. Everything starts to swim. There's a loss of picture quality and the tang of salt. And I'm not alone in this. Something melts in us – as we are honoured after long days' walking. Reassured that this endeavour is worthwhile. Has value.

Áurea was right. The blessing is indeed meaningful, the emotion heightened near the end of this pilgrim road.

Semi-shocked, we file into the still evening air, reluctant to shatter the spell with speech and dissolve the mystery. But we do.

Wandering back to the Albergue I fall in with two of the late arrivals, Nuno and Judy, he Portuguese, she Nigerian, who have walked the Camino da Costa from their Atlantic front door in Labruge. Having had three children in five years, they needed time together to get to know each other again.

'It was ten days either in New York or the Camino,' Judy says. 'I've always longed to do it but never knew why. Until now.'

'The forest back there,' Nuno says, 'was special. The peace ...' his voice trails away, he shakes his head in disbelief.

'And the Vespers,' Judy adds. 'That place had such energy, emotion.'

I mention about Ero's legend.

'You could almost believe it,' she says.

Over coffee in the Albergue, they surprise me with their question, 'What is the story of James?'

I relate a little of his legend – as inner circle disciple of Christ, then apostle to Iberia, and of his martyrdom and the Translatio return to Galicia, 'But it's the fact that so many have walked there for over a millennium ... that's important for me. His remains might or might not be in Santiago.'

'I hope the Legend's true,' Judy says.

Nuno says, 'They say if you walk around Santiago Cathedral three times, you will see everyone you met on the journey. Perhaps we will.' And we did.

* * *

In the Albergue it's 3:00 a.m. I'm wide awake in this place of deep Celtic connections with home. My mind races, replaying yesterday's conversations and events. 'Three years ago,' I'd told Áurea, 'I arrived in Armenteira by accident on San Ero's feast day.'

'Perhaps it was Providence,' she'd said.

For sure it's been a place of fascination ever since.

Then I come to realise that Ero's legend is not mere fantasy, but a metaphor – on multiple levels. And thoughts tumble out onto notebook pages.

Ero wanders deep into the forest: symbol for the soul's depths, into the 'First Book of God,' transported through Nature to bliss, to enchantment, in a didactic tale of Panentheism: the divine presence residing both within *and* beyond Nature.

For as John Muir, the Scottish-American ecologist and author maintained, each journey out is really a journey in – to the threshold of where messages pass back and forth.

What was it Áurea said? 'Something wonderful happens when we connect with the mystery within.'

The Ero story rises from a metaphor for the religious life inspired by Celtic Christianity. Just as other stories of deep time were; such as Brendan's Navigatio was, with his seasonal circuits of travel, drawing him closer to source. Ero's three-hundred-year sojourn likewise stands as a Celtic symbol of immersion into Divine consciousness.[42]

For just as Rumi cries out, 'The longing inside is the voice of God. What you seek is seeking you,' so Ero wanders out from religious form and deep into the forest's solitude and hears a song always being sung had we but ears to hear. Enlightened, he returns to the sacred space of the abbey, his feet like Columba's following his heart to the place of his resurrection to know the place as if for the first time

A millennia later his spiritual children, like pioneers, continue to chart an inner landscape, reaching across the porous divide to bring through echoes of the Otherworld, their voices enchanting the land again.

Is this what Áurea really meant by *The Stone and The Story*?

Matins
The rising sun flames the eucalyptus hills red. Swallows rise to scythe the air, their happy fate always to bring spring and summer. I covet one last cloister walk as there's no guarantee I'll be here again.

And as a robin's song line trails away, plainsong drifts out from the chapel, a matins' call-and-response – to an audience of one … precious lives spent in prayer and song, atop a mountain, far from the concerns of the world but holding them ever high – that little bit closer to heaven.

Silvia, my Italian friend from the walk from Porto, comes by, packed and ready to leave. I point to my inclined ear, and we sit together in silence for some moments as song rises from stone.

* * *

Walking into the shade of the Stone and Water Route, I recall Catherine's comparison of the religious life to a river: 'We drop down, immerse ourselves in its flow and let it carry us.'

I imagine her fallen into that furious river known to the lovers of God, carried in its current, her hands outstretched, reaching for balance, as she attends to guests, then returns to the flow – alternating between the mundane and the mystical.

She knows her Thomas Stearns Eliot: 'The river *is* inside us and the ocean all around.' Living water welling up from our Pointe Verge – even as springs rise to become angel echoes, the voice of many waters flowing around this place.

If only my camera could capture the reality behind this veiled place. But like Áurea last year refused to be photographed, we see surface activity but it's all going on beneath, in the flow, where the river roils.

CHAPTER 24

The Río Umia –
River of Dreams, Memories

The Río de Armenteira burbles downhill past moss-covered rocks to join the Río Umia – where the Variante route becomes a riverside walk.

I stop at a sign reminding me that the Umia rises in the parish of Aciveiro, Forcarei. My fingers trace the map line of its course, and I'm transported back to last year, when, on a whim, I decided to follow it from source to sea.

* * *

In a Silleda Hotel's reception, I ask to order a taxi for the morning, to take me to the Monastery of Santa María de Aciveiro.

'Ok,' the woman says, 'It's about twenty minutes away. How long do you want him to wait?'

'No, I'll start walking from there.'

'But that's not the way to Santiago.'

'I know.'

'Why do you want to go there? It's not the Camino.' (Silleda lies on the Vía de la Plata route).

She looks baffled, my behaviour inconsistent with 'foreigner,' and, 'backpack'. Why indeed? I couldn't say. Perhaps I've got this all wrong.

I try to explain that I want to walk not The Camino, but my own route, following the Río Umia to Caldas de Reis and the REia de Arousa. 'It rises between A Reigosa and Filloi, in the parish of ...'

Her raised palm says 'Stop!' Her expression suggests straitjacket. She turns to another desk and asks her boss (doubling as an estate agent) 'Is this so?'

He breaks off from his client, and turns, curious, to confirm that, 'Yes, it rises in the parish of Aciveiro.' Then adds, 'No-one has ever asked about this before.'

She relents, makes the booking, and I'm released to wander through Silleda's golden hour.

Outside a café bar, nuts crack like crickets' wings over tables. Plates fill with splayed shells as Tapas is served: anchovies draped on oval pieces of bread, then savoury treats, yellow, shining.

Louis from home rings and asks where I am. This time. I tell him, and he says, 'Where?'

* * *

In the morning, the taxi arrives for a twenty-minute ride to the Monastery of Santa María.

The hotel's owner accompanies me outside and asks Artur to look after me, as I might be a little...' Then I lose the word. Perhaps it was, 'confused'.

Soon we are in pastoral countryside.

'Beautiful here,' I say, '*Muy Tranquilo. Paz y tranquilidad.*'

Artur looks askance, shakes his head and murmurs, 'Much too much *tranquilidad.*'

'I prefer the city,' he says.

What he despairs of, I crave. He lived in Madrid for nine years, returning last year to his father's business.

The further we climb through purple heather hillsides and past moorland, the more his mood darkens, the wheel clenched knuckle tight, the place hanging heavier on him. Field after field, like life, passing him by.

Above, vague ridgelines and a glimpse of windmills stir the mist of hill farm country. Its peoples everywhere taciturn, hardy, possessed of a quiet dignity born of endurance in a place of unanswered prayer.

We crest a hill and he points to a quadrant of buildings below. 'There's Aciveiro.' Terracotta tiled rooftops above the mottled stone. A church, cloister and monastery.

He stops before its porch, it's twelfth-century Romanesque purity mutilated by a Baroque eighteenth-century facade. We step out into the sharp slap of cold air.

He assesses the place, shudders, hands me my pack and his card.

'If you need to, ring me,' he stresses, 'and I'll come and get you.'

He drives off; I'm left alone. The iglesia's quartet of bells is silent. Only a crow cawing as rain glistens on granite. It's now my turn to shiver and check my phone. No signal.

Two miniature holly trees frame the entrance porch. At this altitude, they are everywhere, the parish named after one species: Acivro.

Once immersed in a vast forest, the monastery was one of fifteen sown throughout Galicia at the height of the Pilgrimage and Castilian imperial designs.

I press and re-press the intercom for a chance to walk the cloister, but no one is yet at home in this place now re-tasked as a summertime *pousada*.

The rain eases – mist thins. So I sit for a moment on a stone seat beneath a *cruceiro* to check my maps. Then start walking north, past pollarded ash, and ancient, moss-covered Holm Oaks. Rills and runnels burble over grassy banks, raindrops pearl on lattice wire fences. Past ash keys hung like Santiago crosses and see-through mists of green forming on poplar branches. To where the streams of Raigosa, Filloi, Alende and Grela merge, and the Umia is born.

* * *

At A Reigosa, I ignore a 'No Trespassing' sign and, witnessed by a scarecrow's accusing gaze, step over the red and white crime-scene tape and into a marshy meadow, its spongy earth springing back into place after minefield footsteps.

Suddenly, a stream beneath a hedgerow matches my map. I wander along the ditch, following until it emerges from under a bank. But another stream runs into it. Then more runnels rising. Perhaps there is no one precise source.

In the next field, beyond a screen of trees, a tractor slow-growls. Wanting assurance I am in the right place I wave to the farmer and his wife.

He is dispatched to challenge and stands at a gap in the hedgerow, a spade in his hand.

I apologise for my trespass then, as I explain my intention, his face relaxes, and he spikes the spade into the ground and nods.

'This is the place, isn't it?' I ask.

'Yes. This field – this is the start.' Then turning he continues, 'But it's all the Umia here. All around.'

And as he speaks, his hands pass palms down over the earth, as if they could sense a sea of silvery liquid beneath our feet, ready at any moment to break through.

And in those seconds, his coat indigo-blue, the colour of woad, I picture him as a descendent of a Druidic Shaman, his hands charged from a lifetime of field days spent divining the unseen.

I thank him and return to the road as a light rain begins to seep deep into the earth – even as rainfall from decades ago rose, opposing gravity to flow again.

In every direction undulating fields, hills and vales ripple, resting on waters haunting. The land like a seascape rising, falling, and me with it, trying to find my sea legs as I set out to follow the Umia's snaking 70 kilometre course all the way to the ría's silver shimmer.

Rivers of Life

Again I trace the line on the riverside sign, and begin a twelve-kilometre saunter to Pontearnelas, mouthing the names of places become familiar, triggering memories now lodged between the syllables of Forcarei, A Estrada, Caldas de Reis, and Meis.

Long before the place called Galicia was imagined, rivers like the Umia birthed communities by their banks. River roads were the common thread connecting peoples working the fields or casting nets, deeply attached to both land and sea.

For the Galician soul (formed Janus-like from land and seascape) faces both ways, looking to the past as a resource for the future. Its people paradoxical: shy yet proud, reticent then strident, religious yet superstitious, Galician *and* Spanish.

Isn't their cultural stereotype of *Retranca* – an ironical reserve – a classic example of ambiguity, whimsy? Even their national poet, Rosalía de Casatro, couldn't make up her mind: one moment extolling the oak groves by Padrón's Río Sar, then finding herself caught up in Atlantic longing – *Abrideme a ventana que quero ver o mar* …Open up my window and let me see the sea – daubed on walls and pavements.

And we are similarly drawn to river and ocean, to places numinous in every culture, to settings that soothe, cleanse, and restore.

Our oldest metaphor is a garden, but one with a river running through it. Celts once believed that the earth floated on water, its bubbling up from the ground revered as holy mystery, as a blessing. Hence all those holy wells.

For Jungians, for Christians, rivers symbolise the Unconscious, or the soul. Baptists stood in them, mid-western revivalists gathered by them, while Jewish exiles wept remembering Zion.

The healing temples of ancient Greece were sited by rivers and springs. Hindus credit them with being inherently holy. And, at the end of our journeying, we're ferried across Styx or Jordan.

Our language and thought abound with words and images freighted with river metaphors. Thoughts are cherished when the internal 'dam breaks' and they free-flow, course, glide, gush, rush or pour onto the page in 'streams of consciousness'. But when the flow ceases, our heads spin, our thoughts whirl-pool.

Rivers continue to fascinate our poets and writers: Springsteen went down to one, as a symbol of timeless connection and healing; Dylan sat by another, transfixed by its flow; others sought a frozen river as a means to skate away on; or, like Norman MacLean, compose *A River Runs Through It*, his Unitarian poem to purity.

But perhaps their deepest metaphorical linkage is with time: speeding by or moving slowly. Who indeed knows where the time goes?

Healing Waters
The chimes from Ribadumia's Bell Tower bring me back to the moment, back to the river. My phone *and* a waymark tell me that an hour has passed in what seemed like minutes.

Woodsmoke drifting blues the air as my steps disturb a giant, lean bird on the far bank, one as if time-slipped from prehistory. With a resentful glance, the heron unfurls its silver-grey wings, rises imperious, then slow-rows east, to where the valley stretches out before me.

I sit on a bench to watch the río slide by, glinting silver, one of the thousands that once powered the mills that fed a world.

Now the energy flows from hilltops as the wind turns the blades that sail this delicately balanced lifeboat through the void.

All the grids trace back to a wheelhouse where a crew, drunk on dominion and set on a redesign, grind the gears that hurl steel and concrete high to Babel the sky. Their ears stopped to the *rivers that mine the silence of stone*, that burble out their logos language.

And yet, the veins of the earth run in resistance still, by wildflower meadows, yellow and purple, as birdsong choirs bring the good news of doors left unlocked.

Amid the Elysian Fields of O Salnés, I visualise parents, aunts and uncles now lost to sight walking the meadow, impossibly young again, their steps lighter, their cares and crosses sloughed off, as if dipped by a God in restoring waters.

I both reach out to them yet carry them with me.

Some say our stories began near the sound of water; mine overlooking Belfast's River Lagan, the route settlers moved along to found a city. Now the Camino has led me to a similar river, where the trees reach over from each bank to almost touch.

Beside me a Mayfly, golden-brown, hovers. It gestates for years underwater before surfacing to moult and live for only a day or two. Their glide across water is said to represent a gaze beneath the surface of things. For us, also, so much lies beneath the conscious, with only a Jung here, or a Freud there, to guide.

Late in the afternoon I arrive in Pontearnelas, with its thick stone houses and terracotta roofs.

A little temple, the Capilla de Santa María, sits forlorn and silent with its empty chairs, fresh posies and lace-wrapped sweets as votive offerings beneath its white draped altar.

The Umia is spanned by a Roman bridge, since topped with cobblestone and wrought iron railings. Known as the Godparents

Bridge, Legend says that a woman having difficulty conceiving or at risk of a miscarriage, was advised to wait here in silence. The first man to cross on foot is asked to baptise the woman's stomach with water from the Umia. If pregnancy results, the man becomes the child's godfather.

Perhaps this alludes to greater intimacy than water baptism. Here, fertility legends linger long.

My legs stiffening, I watch dark water slide over a weir – the pane of its glassy flow unbroken. As if it could also carry cares away.

A family sheath their phones and stare – the water's hush a finger to their lips. Such stillness echoes elsewhere: St Jean Pied de Port in the French Pyrenees, where other Camino journeys begin, where the Nive also flows under a Roman Bridge and over weirs. I sit on the bank as a man in a thick brown corduroy coat shuffles past, his face a weather-beaten match under a shock of black hair, a sickle in his right-hand.

Above, other scimitar silhouettes scythe the air – as swifts scream and dart past. It's been said that their flight, 6,000 miles to and from Southern Africa to moult and breed, threads the world together. Perhaps Camino walking does with ours, with mine.

The same movements in the skies as when Roman Legions marched here to wrest control from Celtic tribes. Far from Rome's madding crowds to where fresh winds blew rumours of eternal youth from healing spas.

And they brought with them their stolen gods, gifted from Greece. One, Asclepius, relocated from his shrine at Epidaurus to heal a plague in Rome.

This child of Apollo and a mortal, tutored by the wise centaur Cheiron in the curative arts, was murdered by a jealous Zeus, then raised from the dead to become a divine, wounded healer.

In ancient Greece, if I had sickness in body or soul, I'd consult an Asclepian healer for a herbal remedy. But if these failed, there was a final possibility: a sacred journey to one of the God's healing temples, all somewhat grander than the Capella de Santa Maria; all of them set in remote places, and always by the soul symbols of rivers or springs.

On arrival, I would bathe in ritual purification, engage in a cathartic conversation with a priest, then wait, perhaps for days, in a special chamber, an *incubatum*, for a healing dream – sent by the God himself.[43]

One might say that the healing path laid down by the ancient Greeks continues to be a model for the soul, with its recommendations for pilgrimage, purification, catharsis, introversion and healing dream.

This tradition was later adopted by the Greek Orthodox Church and required one to travel with family members churches dedicated to St Cosmo and St Damian – their twin healing saints – where they slept and awaited the healing dream. This practice also occurred in Sufi and shamanic cultures, where guidance as to how to make the unconscious (collective or otherwise) conscious was valued.

On Pilgrimage, dreams tend to be more vivid because, once one has been prised away from the familiar, one learns more clearly that the movement towards wholeness occurs not through assent to a set of intellectual beliefs – but, rather, through what the pilgrim Ignatius termed 'motions of the soul', little 'consolations', that move us to better places.

I wonder might we dare to believe that the Camino's call is part of the greater healing dream of a wandering unlicensed Rabbi with his vision of community, inclusion, and the suspension of judgement?

* * *

Swifts again stream past, heading west, taking my reverie with them. This year they've screamed and careened over rooftops all the way north from Porto.

I get up to stretch stiff limbs, then remember that poets like Rilke and RS Thomas stress that the point of travel: '… is not to arrive, but to return home laden with pollen you shall work up into the honey the mind feeds on'.

So, mindful of their words, I make a phone call and begin a slow-step return to Ribadumia, for tonight I want to stay by the river to see what else it might whisper.

On the way I gather more memories: of two boys that run, shout then jump from a pontoon, twisting in the air to look back; of blackbirds trampolining the path – jumping for joy; of fishermen silently stalking their prey, teasing lines as they wonder why nothing is happening.

In my six years of Camino wandering, often, at the end of a day, a deep sense of connection arrives. Like tonight.

I wonder why this sensation is so elusive. Does it have to be earned by long days of walking through places of overwhelming beauty? Is that what brings temporary release from the ticker-tape ream of anxious thoughts, that permits those minutes of heightened awareness and an intense focus on the moment?

A Dream and a Blackbird singing

In Ribadumia's hostel, in my own room, after a shower, I stretch out on the bed. Almost there. In the morning, Mouzos, Vilanova and the Ría de Arousa where the *Bateas*, the mussel rafts, lie sleeping, summer lounging, their endless work also carried out below the surface.

Sinking deeper into the sheets, my eyes closed, I play on a loop the soundtrack to this trip, Will Reagan's *Pilgrim Days*.[44] Its entreaty? That we join in song as we walk each other home.

And I imagined straggled lines of people in cloaks, shawls, in torn tee-shirts or tattered suits, clutching cardboard suitcases close to their chests. Others journeying through twilight seasons, from east and west, from desert, savannah, mountain and plain: the saints of the road.

Then somehow, I was amongst them to see that each band was led not by the rich, powerful or pious, but by storytellers, the picaresque voices of the ages. The outsiders, the people of the edge, appointed not for their correct beliefs but rather because it was the integrity of their search that counted.

Some were Orwellian prophets, speaking truth to power. Others, poets transposing into words the hopes and longings of peoples, passing fresh pages to singers and musicians. For each group had their own troubadours of travel.

Some danced as if before an Ark, playing harps, harmoniums, drums and guitars; others charmed with pipes, flutes, fiddles, lutes, their music rising from each winding caravan. Faster than thought, harmony flowed from dextrous fingers – phrase layered upon phrase.

Each took the lead, then gave way – and like jazz virtuosos shouted encouragement to the next, then muttered to themselves and each other, 'I've never played like that before – or heard *him* play so well.'

Some slowed their step to console the weary. For others, it was the song of a lark that lifted their bowed heads.

But, in my dream, I was still foot-draggingly weary, and kept falling behind, my eyes half-closed.

Then others stopped, staring at something in the half-light. They rubbed their eyes in disbelief and pointed ahead. The image that now cleared was shaped like a distant city, its towers stretching high … and, behind them, something like the dawn.

Each group slowly straightened at this sight, before their steps quickened again. Sure-footed, their strength increased as the weight of years fell away. As they grew younger. The dust of the journey becoming sheen on their clothes, glittering like Starfield quartz in granite.

The more they'd endured, it seemed, the greater they shone.

And there were tears. Tears that cleared the eyes of the heart. For tears and joy came from the same place – from a sweet melancholy become bliss.

As they approached the city's gates, drum beats quickened, step and song became more urgent. But even as the musicians, one by one, put their instruments away, the music remained, as if somehow, *they* had become the song.

For each group, the dawn broke again and again as they passed through the gates.

More than anything, I wanted to walk in with them. But I was falling further behind. Running and running, in slow motion, never gaining, as if on a reverse walkway.

I fell, got up breathless, and fell again, as a siren klaxoned, shaking the plain. My chest now tight with fear that the gates might shut, and I'd be left outside.

The image faded and I was torn away to a cell's darkness, or a room I didn't know, while a car horn blared outside, the clock blinking 3:00 A.M., the taste of salt on my tongue and the words singing out something about Jubilee, and chains undone.

I tore my headphones off as the car raced away, leaving only the sound of raindrops pattering through the darkness. Then a blackbird, somewhere, singing.

CHAPTER 25

Mouzos and the Chapel of San Pedro

Close now to Mouzos. Over the Puente Santa María, and past riverbank willows. This year … gone in a flash, like the swallows skimming the road ahead. Soon they'll leave, towing the dreams of summer south.

Time speeding up even as it counts down. Summer shortening, gone like the bluebirds. They know what we don't, and need – the rhythm of back and forth, birthing new hope. Something novel to slow the sand-glass flow.

Again, the Celtic quandary of souls riven by a love of home and the need to wander. Trying to stretch out time by splicing in fresh footage.

Sometimes it feels like we've been cast out into the night and asked to find our way home again, with only star fields to guide us, or whispered prayers borne on the wind, flayed from the lips of poets with anguished hearts, or the words of wild men wandering in coarse clothing, fed on honey cake and desert silence, leaving a crumb here and there.

Through Pontearnelas, there's a gap in the clouds and a trick of the light. Slanted sunbeams falling on three pilgrims tip-tapping their way across the sigh of cobblestone bridge. For a moment, everything slows and merges into one, as if this place passes through them, rather than they through it.

Is that the difference between tourist and pilgrim? Not skimming over the surface but immersed so deeply in a landscape that some of it lodges and never falls away? Is that how a name on a map becomes a place in the heart?

This place, the whole of O Salnés, is like a babushka doll. With each visit, I discover more treasures hidden within.

Another straggled line on the road ahead, called by their own primal instincts, backpacks and scallop shells flapping, venturing out from east of Eden, course set for a field of stars – to catch one falling, perhaps.

I hear poet John O'Donohue whisper, 'Listen to the new silence brought with them'. These fragile hearts made restless by the fault in our gene pool, our stars or echoes of eternity layered in. Each step scattering their song lines, dreaming in the land of their sojourn.

If one spent a lifetime wandering these paths it wouldn't be a waste. Treading softly on the dreams of pilgrims who went before them, shaking out and folding tents in the desert, moving on. The Stone and Water Route shimmering, as Manley Hopkins might say, 'like shook foil'.

Then sudden shapes everywhere, as swallows and martins burst out, shot from God knows where, weaving, flashing past on final feeding runs before their long migration.

The road winds uphill, past the sculpture of a boy bent over his school desk peering intently at a Celtic spiral, trying to divine its meaning. Opposite is a junior football ground. I think I know where he'd rather be.

A Variante sign takes me left, to Río Pequeño, Mouzos and the Chapel of San Pedro. To meet Alfonso Cherene. He and his wife Debee have begun working with residents of the village of Mouzos, in opening the Chapel to passing pilgrims. As he greets me, another man slowly rises from the porch, leaning heavily on his stick. He blinks as I shake his hand. Don José. His son Jaime soon joins us.

'Before we had a stamp,' Alfonso explains, 'Don José would plant his stick in ink and stamp the pilgrims' passports.'

José nods; his stick is now decommissioned by a scallop shell stamp.

Shading the porch is a camellia tree, with its symbolism of the Divine, the promise of spring, the passing of winter. A plaque on the wall records that the chapel was built in 1978, the year of the new constitution, of new democratic beginnings – the coming of spring again to Spain. The start of the *pacto del olvido* – of forgetting wrongs. I tell him that camellia also celebrates faithfulness, longevity. He nods.

Over time, as more images and icons were brought to the chapel, Jaime expanded the chapel even as the village population declined, the tradition of family farming ebbing as children sought new opportunities or sold the land and moved away. The lot of rural communities everywhere, this loss of a special connection to the land.

'Then three years ago,' Alfonso tells me, 'Don José, Jaime and others lobbied for the Camino to go through the village. The mayor later told me it was the only issue they ever sought a meeting on.'

And it brought new life. Few in Mouzos have travelled widely, but now the world walks by their front doors, along laneways, and through farmyards and small vineyards. The disappointment of ageing patriarchs is eased by the flow of new pilgrim generations, with their appreciation of sacred space and reverence for the beauty of the land.

Now there are greetings, drinks, fruit shared. And for Jaime, appreciation of the work of his hands – the chapel his legacy. I ask him to explain something of the images and icons inside. He leads me to a San Blas here, attentive to prayers for the throat, a Virgin of Guadalupe there, with her miracle cures. To the side, Fátima – 'My father wanted this image,' he says – and in the centre, an image of San Pedro above Christ crucified.

They will keep this place open every day until the boat stops sailing daily at the end of the first week in November, and next year from Easter onwards.

Then pilgrims are at the doors, edging into the church. Alfonso rises to greet them. Jaime moves to follow, taking his place with his father, stamping pilgrim passports, listening to their stories of the day's walk.

I sit awhile, savouring the atmosphere, thinking of the many for whom this section has been the highlight of their Camino Portugués. Their comments in the visitors' book, messages of gratitude for 'hospitality', 'love', 'peace', and 'welcomes like shining stars'.

A pine-clad ceiling. White walls. White carnations on a simple altar. And underneath, a holy nativity family. The shepherds have been and gone, the wise men yet to set out, journeying from afar.

Her head tilted, Mary gazes on the child, lost in wonder. Joseph leans on his staff, perhaps wondering at hope arriving as a vulnerable babe, entrusted to the poor and obscure, the least the first to hear – creating a whole new set of haves and have nots. Or perhaps he's thinking, 'What the heck do I do now?'

I ask the same question of the Carpenter Messiah. Who else has the words? Some of them echo still, embodied here in hands that build and hearts that greet.

Outside, laughter breaks the spell. More pilgrims pass by, written into the Camino's story, even as it rewrites ours, telling us who we still could be. They walk on to Santiago, but never really arrive. None of us do. Then travel home, but never really return.

* * *

A car arrives. The driver gets out and beckons us over.

'He has some wine to give us,' Alfonso says.

I reach out to shake Manolo's red-stained hand.

He opens his boot, full of flagons.

'Take as much as you want. I have to make a fresh batch. Of Barrantes wine. It has a very full taste. No chemicals or preservatives added.'

We sample it. He's right. We sample again – just to make sure.

'Smooth, full-bodied,' I say.

'Yes, but not as strong as Albariño. You should stop walking, take a day off, put your feet up and enjoy a bottle.'

'But if I do that, I may miss my flight.'

He smiles and says, 'Then you must come back.'

CHAPTER 26

The Island of Cortegada

(Opposite the fishing village of Carril – Vilagarcía de Arousa)

Silence at low tide. A shoreline blueprint of stone squares and rectangles, then hundreds of tar-black poles driven deep, as if about to cast long lines across sparkling sea to Cortegada, five hundred metres away.

Men in chest-high waders and waist-high water plunge cockle rakes into sediment.[45]

Handles grasped in both hands, leaning back in a tug-of-war pose, they work the rake back-and-forth, as if loosening a giant molar. Slowly filling the cage with the extracted catch. Scraping a living.

There's a sound like waves creeping over shingle as cockles and clams are tipped alive into buckets buoyed by rubber rings – then dragged to *Gamelas*: the flat-bottomed, square-sterned boats in which women sort according to value.[46]

Brendan and I stand watching. An elderly man in a blue fisherman's hat, leaning over the seawall, casts a weather eye on the efforts below. We ask him about the poles and stones on the beach.

They are demarcation lines for plots owned by different families. His friend has just spent €5,000 on tiny cockles which, seeded into beds for six weeks, will then be re-planted and grown in larger plots – shoreline horticulture in the sweet spot where salt and fresh water meet, close to the mouth of the Río Ulla and its rich nutrients.

'Good for shellfish,' he says, 'and the lower tides this far up the ría means there's more sun on the flats.

'These factors make Carril clams and mussels 'famous, and more expensive.'

He points to boats a little further out, with rakes over the stern. '*They* are fishing for *Almejas*.' (clams)

'Are the razors there also?' I ask.

'No, no.' He shakes his head at a question only an amateur would ask.

'Those are out in the ría, ten or fifteen metres deep down in the cold, and hand-picked by divers using oxygen tanks. They look for a hole in the sand, put salt down and when the clam comes up ...' a pause as he grasps the air. 'Caught! The diver's hands are covered in cuts. They can't use gloves.'

We tell him that no-one at the dock will take us across.

'Of course, they won't. They are far too busy right now, working in the low tide. But look,' he points to a man wading with a rake and shouldering a bucket. 'Look where he walks. Do you see it?'

Barely visible under the water is something like a cobble-stone track from the shore.

The Island of Cortegada and The Way of the Cart

'You can cross there – on El Camino Del Carro.' (The Way of the Cart).

He shrugs and says, 'You might have ninety minutes – at most.' He then steps back from the wall as if from an altar but remains stooped double as he walks to his car.

Even as we turn to each other, it's already decided. We'll wade across The Way of the Cart to the largest laurel forest left in Europe, to a place of dreams and visions, history and healing, wars and rumours of wars.

We emerge from knee-to-thigh-high water onto a desiccated shell beach and follow cartwheel tracks grooved into a stone path through oak and pine – to the remains of a village clustered on the island's south-east corner, the place of greatest sunlight and maximum shelter from the north winds.

For millennia, a community bustled here, peering through eastern windows and a screen of trees out to the ria. Their houses are now reduced to roofless remnant walls, moss and ivy-covered, sinking down into earth. Yet, set into them, there's a trace of a water trough here and a bread oven there.

I wonder how bitter their last supper was, and when and why the village was abandoned?

On the island's western shore, the fourteenth-century church of the Virgen de Los Milagros (Virgin of Miracles) retains only its frontal facade, propped up by beams.

In the Middle Ages, the sick came to Cortegada seeking relief in great numbers, raising the risk of infection so high that in 1652, the chapel was dismantled, stone by stone, moved from the village and rebuilt here. A *Lazaretto* (a small hospital for the care of leprous pilgrims) was added, a pioneering effort at quarantine long before San Simon.

The resident monks (seconded from Santiago's Benedictine San Martín Pinario monastery) were well aware of the healing potential of this forest pharmacy. They used willow bark (containing salicin, eventually used in Aspirin) to treat fevers; alder leaves served as poultices for insect bites or aching feet; boiled oak leaves addressed gastric problems, while hawthorn reduced high blood pressure. But their specialist subject were remedies for stomach illnesses, utilising the five hundred varieties of laurel they propagated.

Their pioneering homeopathic, holistic care system, famed throughout the region, had them collecting seaweed along the shore to remedy rheumatism, or shepherding those with skin conditions into the salty waves. (Four hundred years later, the benefits of sea bathing have suddenly come back into fashion.)

133

Beyond the shore, cormorants stand on rocks with wings transfigured after heavy dining while, further out, the sea swallows, arctic terns, scream out their stories.

A man in a Ranger's uniform approaches during his circuit of the island, and intrigued by my questions about Cortegada's history, walks me back to pick up leaflets at his office – past where a defence tower once stood.

'Cortegada belonged to the Bishop of Santiago.'

'Like so much land here.'

'Yes. You saw the village. But the rest of the island was once intensely cultivated with maize, potatoes, rye and wheat.'

At his hut, he opens a huge tome which contains a diagram of its nineteenth-century usage – in what looks like a mass of cricket strips and squares crammed together.

'Then, a thousand plots fed not only the village families but others coming from the mainland. The soil was so good.'

A thousand plots and a thousand years of village life. '*Minifundio*,' I say.

'Yes,' he echoes, '*Minifundio*.'

Something of its legacy survives in myriad vegetable gardens. But the practice dispersed ownership and reduced power by breaking land use down into small plots, keeping people economically dependent.

'How many tenants did the Bishop have?' I ask.

'70,000 vassals at one time.' His right eyebrow rises.

'Almost Feudal.'

'Yes. He amassed great wealth from high rents and spent a lot of it on church property and decor.'

I later heard someone speak of Minifundio as paying for the 'Baroquefication' of Santiago, stifling investment and Galician development, limiting urbanisation, and reinforcing its geographical and rural isolation.

'Just paying the rents meant hard work and long hours,' he says. 'Villagers were forced to make their living from both land *and* sea.'

But the start of the 20th century brought change.

'There was a campaign to get wealthy locals to purchase the island and gift it to King Alphonso XIII, as a site for his summer residence.'

An attempt to curry patronage and building contracts, I suggest.

He nods. 'In 1907, it was bought from the Bishop and the villagers evicted. There were fifteen families then, about two hundred people. When it was donated to the king three years later, he'd already built his summer home in Santander. This place became part of his hunting grounds.'

Laurel, prone to voracious growth if untended, spread rapidly to re-wild the island.

'In 1931, the Second Republic took control and built an outpost here. Then Franco transferred it back to the Bourbons. Eventually, in 2007, the regional government bought it … for €70 million I think.'

He checks his watch, looks to Carril and tells us, 'You need to leave. Now.'

But we steal a march to the *cruceiro* on the Isla's north-eastern corner (the first of 17 on a Via Crucis marking the James legend of return). And take a final look along the estuary: the same view that Bronze Age settlers had, that Celt, Greek, Roman, Viking and Pilgrim enjoyed – across sky-borrowed blue to a horizon framed by the Barbanza mountains, north, and Mount Castrove, south.

So many stories lie compacted in these fifty-four hectares: of peoples, empire, plague and pilgrimage, of wealth extracted from villagers at the mercy of the powerful, of the great and the not so good. Then eviction and re-wilding, as the story comes full circle on this place in between.

The rushing tide rises to waist high as we wade back. I stumble, step off the track and am told off by a *Marinero* for my trespass on his cockle bed.

Back again in a different world, past to present, we sit soaked but happy outside a smoke-filled Saturday bar, and look back to a densely wooded place of slumber. Then scroll through our photos – and they remind of Welsh poet RS Thomas's phrase about travel bringing the hope of gathering 'snapshots of the garden of the spirit,' stealing … 'another lock of God's hair, while he was asleep'.

* * *

Tomorrow, on the Boat to Pontecesures, there will be coffee, magdalenas, wine, and a flurry of statistics from its owner, Santi: that there are 2,200 Bateas (Mussel rafts) in the Ría de Arousa alone.

'Each Batea, with 500 ropes dangled twelve metres beneath the surface carries as much as 200 kilos of mussels on each cable.'

The boat will come in close, to let us watch the automated lift, strip and wind of each – even as cockle rakes continue their plunge into shoreline silt. The boat's engine will open up as a pod of dolphins track us; as a mallard furiously paddles to escape our prow; as a heron's wingbeats skim the water's surface.

We'll learn that during the March and September equinox, with the pull of the moon and the position of the sun, the ria is only one metre deep. We could walk across, almost, on water.

And we'll stop behind Cortegada, on the North East corner, where we stood today, to mark the first of the Translatio route's twelve crosses – its Christ figure, as on all the crosses, facing towards the main route to Santiago.

So we'll follow His gaze, set for a city of spires dreaming. Ahead, one more march to a place in between, where you never really arrive, and from which you travel home, but never really return.

SECTION 7
Thoughts from Home and Abroad

CHAPTER 27

The River Lagan

We leave the Camino but it never leaves you. The tables turn. For just as its woodland paths and riverside tracks once reminded us of home, from now on cherished places evoke the faraway.

Whilst walking the Rio Umia, its resonance with Belfast's River Lagan had brought a sense of reaching out to family gone ahead amidst moments of heightened awareness.

So after I got home, I walked again along the River Lagan, one of those familiar places that seem to function as what Richard Mabey calls 'an external memory'.

And on this August evening, the Lagan brought further liminal moments … when time seemed to dissolve and offer a glimpse of the past. When, before my time, I imagined my father, decades ago, also by the river.

Annadale 1953
You'd already walked from the Belfast Telegraph Stone in the city centre to Morning Star bar, south onto the Ormeau – place of the elms; and past the Holy Land's terraced warrens to *yours*, a golden mile of tree-lined river.

Then West, where plane trees, rooftops, chimney-pots, spires and funnels rise to round-topped hills. Soon the sun would melt into

Black Mountain and scatter its crimson-yellow train across the sky. 'Golden Hour,' she says, when sun and troubles melt.

The Lagan's swirling patterns glitter as you cross Ormeau Bridge, the scent of fresh-cut grass and heat rising. It's travelled forty miles, this river, rising at Slieve Croob, gathering strength, enlarged by many streams before wall of basalt turns it east, where it birthed Belfast.

You look across to where the Lagan flows through the city's heartbeat, past warehouse, wharf and dock, to the mouth of the river. It took you away once, to France. A part of you never returned.

The trees lean in, as if listening. And you, also. Once a ferryman plied his trade here, then, in your father's time, it froze and said nothing for weeks.

In this place of boundaries between counties, peoples, them and us, what might the river whisper? That there is only Us?

You look up as other voices spark the air: swallows, more than you've ever seen, tracing out invisible ridge-lines, hills and vales, on their final flights of the day. Streamers charged with electricity, they quiver with joy, and are gone.

You stand entranced, by heights of freedom and this glass-smooth flow – and allow the possibility that even your broken places might yet set.

The river always finds a way, when blocked here, it turns there.

Might you also, you think, as you walk upstream past railings painted corporation-green, between ridgeway and embankment slopes, carved out by men with blue hands and thin coats – for Outdoor Relief.

Ahead, a grammar school of tin and asbestos sheeting has risen – a place fit for well-scrubbed working-class sons. Perhaps even yours, if you ever have one. Its school song is *De Brevitate Vitae* (on the shortness of life). Something never believed by the young; only the old.

A megaphone cyclist barks out time. A single scull slides past as if on a speed lane – to Annadale's suburban views for council rent.

On the far bank, ash and oak turn to flame as a grey heron rises up and over Kings Bridge, like blest bread lifted to sky. And peace steals in, some sense that all will be well, that the loss adjustors of the soul might yet reimburse.

In this place of sweet melancholy, you watch willows glance-touch the water's dark flow, as you slow-walk through the still air, and know, that despite all the wrong turns taken, love still waits.

This Friday night – when the key swells up and won't fit the lock – your wife will retread the hall and open the door to tea, bacon, and bread taken as the houseboats peer back.

For now, the ferryman must wait.

Soon enough, she'll place discs on eyes, for your journey to the other shore.

You don't know it yet, but tonight a boy child will begin, and, like you, be born overlooking the river, within sight of the sea, and watch its flow through holy land. As all becomes one.

CHAPTER 28

Remembrance and Mount Santiaguiño, Padron (on the Central Route)

Though home for Winter, I'm still thinking of Galicia –
Pensando en Galicia.

Cold sunlight floods Belfast's Cenotaph. It's Remembrance Day. Cadets in desert khaki line the way. The beat of a single snare echoes, and ceremony begins.

The pipe and brass band march past to the strains of 'The Star of the County Down' – the same jaunty tune that stepped others away to Picardy and Flanders. The ones that returned stood here year after year on November mornings remembering what could not be spoken of.

A few hundred of us mark this time. A mere two decades ago, these grounds and surrounds were tight-packed. This morning, only a few hundred of us gather.

Elgar's muted strains rise through the air as wreaths are laid for departed Bands of Brothers. Politicians and dignitaries file back slowly, sobered in twin-step choreography with opponents, speaking softly, managing the optics, bringing cold comfort.

Twenty years since this city began its long march away from the sound of the guns only for peacemaking to freeze. And it's not only *our* politics that seem broken.

About to leave, my memory takes me back to an autumn week in Galicia, touring O Salnes with my wife – all dreamy days, toes burrowed into golden sands, the ria glinting, wine tasting, and a final stop in Padrón.

On his feast day, a statue of Saint James is carried across the Santiago Bridge to the 'Escaleras Santiaguiño,' and up 125 steps to a cathedral of oak and pine, to a scatter of stone tables, Edwardian street lamps, and another simple statue of James atop giant boulders. To the site of his first sermon – in an almost Narnian wood between the worlds. A place which I never tire of.

Initially a Celtic Nature Temple, it was Christian-ised in the fifteenth century. It's a place Irish Celtic Christians would feel at home in. For they also gathered outdoors on hillsides and high places, turning the pages of the Second Book of God. They, too, stood before High Crosses carved with bible stories – sermons in stone for the not yet literate. Christ had two feet for balance, they stressed, scripture *and* nature.

We now watch silently as a pilgrim with walking poles and full pack comes panting into view, spots the steps up to the giant boulders and keeps on trekking. Reaching the top, he breathes deep draughts of air, his face filmed in sweat. Then, like a curious bird, his head tics sharply to appraise the miniature statue of James. His face seems to signal 'Is that it?'

His companion arrives. She's hoisted up, and together they raise their arms in a fresh victory salute for another trophy selfie. They loudly talk of the remaining kilometres and are gone a minute later.

* * *

Kay walks to a bench just below to read more of her book. In the prickly heat I settle myself on the carpet of pines needles, my back against a tree trunk's rough bark, close my eyes and listen for what this place might say.

I must have drifted off, because a few minutes later I hear a voice saying, 'Hello Roy, how are you?'

I open my eyes and see a woman I don't recognise standing over me, smiling.

I fluster out, 'I'm good, thank you ...' desperately trying to place her.

'I'm sorry,' I say, getting onto my feet, 'but have we met somewhere?'

Then straightening, she claps her hands, throws back her head and laughs. 'You should have seen your face ... I was talking to your wife below. She put me up to this.'

Christine is from Bremen and has walked from Porto.

She explains: 'We stayed in Herbon last night. But today I wanted to spend some time here – with James. I'd read about this place ... where he preached a mini Sermon on a Mount.

'Tomorrow Santiago. I initially wanted to walk to Finisterre, but I've run out of time.'

I advise her to take the bus out. 'It's the most beautiful coastline I've ever seen. And sit on the left for the sea views.'

'Yes, I'd have time for that. Maybe I will.'

We both have had careers in teaching, and the synchronicity continues as she tells me she too walked the Frances in 2014, the year we both retired.

Our talk shifts to politics.

'We are in trouble back home,' I say. 'So much division and hatred. And our ties with Europe being torn away. Remember what your sage, Goethe, said about the very idea of Europe being birthed on the paths to Compostela? Pray for us.'

'I will.'

'I wish *we* had Angela Merkel as *our* Prime Minister. For her calm, her humanity.'

'Mutti's facing a difficult time,' Christine replies. 'I don't agree with all her policies as I'm a Social Democrat, but she carries herself well, reacts thoughtfully, patiently. Not emotionally. She took a stand in 2015 – letting nearly a million refugees in. "We'll manage this," she said. But that backfired, with the rise of the AFD (Alternative For Deutschland). Now she's in trouble.'[47]

'But she remains a role model for us.'

We both sit and gaze out to the far hillside.

After a few moments, she remarks, 'I think all world leaders need to go on Camino. They'd benefit from getting their feet onto the earth, getting in touch with it so that we can again see each other for who we are.'

'Yes, the real Europe is here, on Camino,' I reply, 'not in Brussels.'

'So much is changing. It's made me just want to walk again,' she says. 'So much stands in danger of being lost. We've forgotten how fragile peace can be.

'My Dad was only twenty-two when he fought at Monte Casino in Italy. Afterwards, he could never talk about it. I've thought of him a lot on this trip. And the things *we* did. Now I want to grieve it all out, so the heartache's not passed on to *my* son.'

She is Catholic. I tell her I am Protestant.

She shrugs. 'It doesn't matter.'

I tell her, '*My* father was also only twenty-two when he fought at Dunkirk. And my grandfather was a young man at the Somme. In different ways, it broke both their health.

'We've made plenty of mistakes in Northern Ireland, things we too need to grieve out.' I tell her how, back in the '90s, I was part of a group that circled Belfast's City Hall, knelt, prayed and repented that our grandfathers, in 1912, had signed The Ulster Covenant. This pledged to resist Home Rule in Ireland by all means, by arms if necessary.

'It was a sort of idolatry – worshipping the idea of a Protestant Ulster, saying, *we* were right; Catholics, Nationalists, were wrong: they believed the wrong things; prayed in the wrong way – politics as a Zero-Sum Game.

'Our ideologies failed. We've had a decade of Anniversaries: 1912, 1916, 1918, and we're still wrestling over their meaning. Too many of us are still looking for the right and wrong side of history. Tragic.'

'I read something about tragedy,' she says, 'that the essence of tragedy is a struggle of right against right. In a tragic struggle, the victors become the guilty and must make amends to the defeated.'

'I wonder then what breaks the stereotype of The Other?'

'Perhaps only acts of kindness,' she says. 'Why else the choice of the Samaritan as Good?'

We've been intensely talking for thirty minutes, as if we'd known each other a lifetime. One gets to know people quickly on the Camino. Stories are shared with near strangers as they never would be at home.

Kay returns and the mood lightens. I suggest that we take a picture of Christine, standing in front of James's statue. 'Then we'll leave you some time with him.'

She clambers up the boulders, throws her arms around the statue and hugs it tightly.

'He's brought me so much, you see. So many friends made on the Camino.'

She climbs down, we embrace, say our goodbyes and walk away.

But before descending the steps, I turn and take a final photo of Mount Santiaguiño as Christine slowly walks around the rocks.

It's been a long road back to the silence observed by my Quaker forebears– and, unexpectedly, via James, the stone vessel into which so many pour their longings. Bringing reassurance that we are not alone. That others experience the same restlessness of heart.

For if James could set out, not knowing where he was bound, then our task may be as simple as to do the next thing – take the next step.

And I think of my ex-soldier grandfather and his passion for gardens, as if they brought some healing memory long forgotten.

On summer evenings, in the stillness of a world far from France, he'd stroll in Belfast's Botanic Gardens, not far from his home, charmed by its pergolas, sunken paths and rose beds that spread fragrant down to the river Lagan.

But one of his contemporaries, Tom Clarke, one of the leaders in Ireland's 1916 Easter Rising, would never experience such evenings.

Lying bleeding in a smouldering post office, a volunteer asked him, 'What would you do if we won?'

'I'd get a small cottage with a big wall around it and grow flowers.'

I wonder that if they'd both lived long enough, might they have come to agree with Alexander Solzhenitsyn, that, 'The line separating good and evil passes not through states, nor classes, nor between political parties – but right through every human heart.' He goes on to explain that this line shifts, oscillates with the years. And that 'even within hearts overwhelmed with evil, one small bridgehead of good is retained. And even in the best of all hearts there remains an uprooted small corner of evil.'

Halfway down, we greet not a Russian but two French-American pilgrims ascending, tired but excited.

'They say the real James is up here,' one says, 'and that this is the best statue of him on the whole Camino.'

I agree. And assure them they will not be disappointed.

'Tomorrow, we finish,' the other says. 'I don't know how I'll feel. I'm worried that Santiago will be tourist trashy. We want to take the peace of the walk back with us.'

Sometimes it can feel like souvenir central, I think, but don't say, then tell them that there's a German lady called Christine who's up there, who's about my height, and wearing a green jacket. 'Say, Hello Christine. How are you?'

* * *

The plane trees by the Rio Sar, which were coppiced last year, have regrown. And the poet Rosalio Castro is remembered. We get a room in the Hotel Rosalia, opposite the train station, and beside her Casa.

It's a room with a view: over furrowed plots, a stand of ash, white tenements, Carmelite convent towers, a hillside bubbled with pine and oak – and a direct line of sight to the roof of the chapel on Mount Santiaguiño.

I love that the statue is hidden by trees. No ostentatious display there, and limited signage. You have to know about it to find it. The terracotta roof is the only visible part of the stone chapel that seems to only open on the 25th of h July. As house for the Holy, a redefined sacred space.

Of course a Patrick or Columba might contend that the real sacred is what surrounds it: the forest church of oak, pine and eucalyptus.

In the evening, lamps light the Mount. And we walk up to be with him again beneath a spill of stars that pulse bright and brighter … a million lights streaming through the veil of night.

CHAPTER 29

Kilbroney, a C.S. Lewis Window and a Celtic Worldview

One August, I began a Camino walk with a visit to St Marks' church in Dundela, east Belfast, before the C.S. Lewis Window, a triptych with an image of St James in its centre and symbols of the Compostela pilgrimage scattered at his feet.

Now, in late November, I'm on my way to Kilbroney Forest Park, Rostrevor, County Down to read at a C.S. Lewis Festival event.

As a boy, Lewis often holidayed there with his family. Decades later, writing to his brother Warnie, he confided, 'That part of Rostrevor which overlooks Carlingford Lough is my idea of Narnia.'

It is a monumental landscape that evokes comparison with Ballinskelligs Bay in Kerry or Galician Rias. And not just for their similar topographies but my suspicion that Lewis's Narnian Myth-making was profoundly influenced by Celtic folk stories.

Growing up, the Lewis children's imaginations were fed by Irish folk tales and legends told by their nurse Lizzie Endicott.

Though Evangelical Protestantism has co-opted Lewis, his personal perspective seems rather more inclusive, nuanced. His father and grandfather may have been ardent Unionists, the latter, Thomas Hamilton, also a fiery, fiercely anti-Catholic Anglican preacher. But there were other views in the family. His grandmother (whom he was close to) and aunt were fervent Home Rulers, belonging to a more Liberal Protestant tradition that once found expression in the 1798 United Irishmen rebellion.

In adulthood, he preferred to plot his own path as a non-aligned Anglican, for years receiving spiritual direction from Anglo-Catholic priest, Fr. Walter Frederick Adams. Politically, his stance was similarly nuanced. He identified himself as 'an Irishman of Ulster,' who decried both Protestant and Catholic sectarian preaching.

In one of his 'Latin Letters' to Don Giovanni Calabria, in 1953, he portrays his birthplace as 'dearest refuge so far as charm of landscape goes, and temperate climate, although most dreadful because of the strife, hatred and often civil war between dissenting faiths.

'There indeed both yours and ours "know not by what Spirit they are led." They take a lack of charity for zeal and mutual ignorance for orthodoxy.'[48]

His choice of the Santiago pilgrimage as the theme for the Lewis Window in St Mark's church, presented by himself and his brother in 1933 in remembrance of their father, was surely an intentionally liberal gesture, given that it was sited in a Protestant east Belfast Anglican church.

* * *

I'm past Newry now. Not far to go. At Narrow Waters Castle canal becomes Carlingford Lough; spindled slopes rise above a north shore of mudflats and salt marshes, winter feeding for the light-bellied brent geese. A woman and child slow-walk on a cemetery-still afternoon. Behind them, a furiously flapping pheasant rises as the sun breaks through.

Landscape often inspires legend. The Tain, the Irish Odyssey originated in the Cooley peninsula, just across the lough.[49]

These glacial sculpted landscapes provided a fitting backdrop for the feats of giants and heroes, from Finn McCool to Cu Chulainn, and from it, perhaps, a Narnian lion later leapt onto the page.[50]

* * *

I arrive early enough to have time to climb Kilbroney's Cloughmore (big stone) trail, all the way up to a fifty-tonne granite boulder. Its dog's head profile stares across to Slieve Foy, from where legend says Finn McCool hurled it at Ruiscaire, mortally wounding his rival Giant of Snow and Ice.[51]

Then the Widescreen HD Narnian view. In the south-east, a lip of land lifts to a round-topped cairn then ascends higher still to where mountain-top crenelles become undulating ridgelines above sheer slopes; slopes that fall into a patchwork of pine forests petering out in a valance of fields that smooth mountain to lough. Where winter sunlight falls on a solitary sail unfurled to catch the wind.

And from above Rostrevor, on this cloud-chasing winter's day, it's easier to understand that what we learn in childhood moulds us most. For so many strands of the *Narnia Chronicles* seem to correspond with Celtic tropes, the Celtic Otherworld becoming replicated in his *Other Worlds*, his Narnian multiverse.

I count off the similarities. How the Celtic Otherworld could be reached through multiple means: by sailing away to western islands; disappearing through elusive and varied portals such as caves, mists, streams, rivers and wells; or by spiritual transport awakened by music and birdsong. All suggesting that nature is riddled with porous places that might at any moment reveal their reality ... rather like Aslan's enigmatic appearances in Narnia – impossible to predict.

The children in the Chronicles also access Narnia via myriad means: through a wardrobe, or by the summons of a Hunting Horn, or a breath of air; by a magic ring; or through a picture of a ship at sea. Or through death. Once they even return through a door in the air.

Reepicheep, the *Dawn Treader's* valiant mouse, even completes his pilgrim journey on board an Irish coracle which bears him up and over a wall of water, the final barrier to Aslan's kingdom.

The relativity of Narnian time is similarly reminiscent of *Immrama* tales, such as The Voyage of Bran, where a year spent on the Island of the Blest amounts to hundreds of our temporal ones.

Also, the imagery highlighted in the 'Narnia Code,' by Michael Ward, would suggest that the colour palette and tone of each book in the Chronicles has been influenced by the properties of different planets. Something which might resonate with studious Druidic observers of the night sky.

Finally, his choice to cast a talking beast as the creator of worlds plainly corroborates the Celtic notion of the sacredness of *all* life. Writ large.

But Lewis couldn't explicitly acknowledge this source of inspiration as that could be interpreted as alignment with one Northern Ireland cultural tradition, when it was his policy to straddle and draw from both. To do otherwise would not have enhanced the career of an Oxford academic in a time of continuing tension between England and the new Irish state concerning its neutrality in the Second World War.

Lewis always preferred the implicit to the blatant. He liked to hide things, a friend said. For years he denied that the Narnia Chronicles were intended as a specifically 'Christian' allegory. As in Celtic myth, much in his writing initially comes across as mystery and enigma – which slowly reveal their meaning.

I retrace my steps through fading light heading to where the Cloughmore Centre glows, dressed to resemble a Winter Wood in Narnia; fir cones and Christmas trees stand against a curtained backdrop of stars and night sky. And to my surprise, I get to read 'A Lewis Window' before a replica of the red door in the vicarage of St Marks, replete with the face of a golden lion. It's a piece imagining his Sunday afternoon childhood visits with his mother to his grandparents in St Mark's Manse on the Holywood Road. And a flight of fancy that follows.

A Lewis Window

> '*The part of Rostrevor which overlooks Carlingford Lough is my idea of Narnia.*'
>
> Letter from C.S.Lewis to his brother

You sit at an Oxford desk staring out to woods. But instead you see the play of light on the hills and shores of home: Cave Hill, Carlingford, then Castlerock and Dunluce with their Atlantic longings. In the power of first impressions on a child's eyes.

Neurons fire. Synapses spark. Messages flash back and forth for moments as blindingly bright as highway headlights. They bring the remembered roar of sea-crash to shore, and the gull's wild call. Then you think to ask *us*, 'Have you heard it? Can *you* remember?'

And you're back at a red door, on Sunday afternoons, your hand in hers, eye level with the burnished brass face of a lion. Red opens to a dim hallway, then to a room furnished with mahogany and glass panels, offering *War and Peace*, *Last Mohicans*, *Water Babies* and buccaneers setting out *Westward Ho*, to the Spanish Main.

Further in, a corridor becomes slipway, leading to portraits of sailboats, rowboats and hide-bound coracles – the past ever-present on unchanging seas. And you there with them. You, who knew about loss – riven by a longing for places not on any map, an Irish Argonaut setting out, rowing about, immersed in *Immrama*. Like a Brendan or a Bran heading west to the Isle of the Blest, from place to the sacred space of horizon events – where waves kiss sky.

Your family tree gives you provenance from Ulster, Wales and Gaul: your farmer, sailor, engineer and clergy forebears stretch back to a Norman Knight. All you'd ever write about was stored up inside, their various strands of dark and light waiting to be woven together.

You draw from these deep and ancient roots *and* the Celtic Otherworld to create your own Other-Worlds. Our transient lands being mere shadow-play to the light and substance of those places out of time.

Your inner Celt invoked, your pen fills with drawn sap and pours onto the page, as you tread the dawn – the template spun from West to Utter-East, as mice and men sail on through salt-damp air.

Until … you picture the Caravel harboured by a shore in snowfall. And she is there also, gone ahead, waiting in the scent of candled green by the door of a clapboard church, its windows aglow.

This inner world fashioned by your words: little scratch marks on paper, syllables sent out to dress the darkness so we may know we are not alone.

Tonight, they fall from somewhere far, falling with and through the snow. The story of each word, like each snowflake, unique; formed around specks of dust seeded to sky to crackle high, their stories carved by the elements of their journey spinning to ground through whited air.

Emotion, now motion-captured, lies lodged between a million snowflakes fallen, born from love's ageless whispers on nights like these to become also part of *our* stories.

Your words, like quantum particles, each reacting differently when observed through the unique experience of the beholder's eye.

Then she turns to you, and says, 'They're always there now. We need only look and listen.'

A bell peals midnight. The great silence breaks. You put down your pen, pad to bed and dream of the Mournes, Downhill, Carlingford and upturned coracles come to rest on another shore.

The double helix constantly spinning out tales, creating order out of chaos. Is that not what storytellers do through hymns to the divinity of imagination?

CHAPTER 30

Belfast, 14th December

We bring our Stories, our home places both to the Camino –
and back.

There's an empty space in the Homebase Christmas display – a hole
in its centre. The floor's being cleared for Spring stock. Eleven days
to go, and it's over before it's over.

Except the memories. Some of a mother widowed far too young.
Whose hands never stopped. Home-working, she sewed for pennies
then curated December displays of paper lanterns midst crisscrossed
ceiling streamers over tinsel-wrapped and star-topped fir, aglow with
perspex angels and reindeers. I have a few reminders, worthless to
all but me: one, a little white plastic Shaker church that once tinkled
out a music box 'Silent Night'. As someone said, *No holiday is holy*
without ghosts. In this season peopled by absences.

* * *

This morning, on television, the journalist Isabel Hardman talked of
her year-long battle with PTSD. Treatment had helped her manage
the symptoms, she said, though a gaping fissure remains. But at least
she'd learnt how to walk around it; to circle the darkness.[52]

Her story reminded me of the Celtic *Caim* (protection) prayer
and its pleading:

'Circle me, Lord, Keep protection near, danger afar.
Keep hope within, and doubt without.'

But what do you do if doubt and danger beat a path to your front door? And seep through every crevice? What if the winter night that has crept inside you squats like dark matter, ice-cold, in the corners of rooms, building strength for its next big push?

Circle it also, step by unsteady step. Keep to the ledge.

* * *

A week from today at Winter Solstice, hundreds will circle Newgrange Passage Tomb, gathered in a conspiracy of hope as a sunbeam creeps along a nineteen-metre passageway into the dark womb of earth.

We go forward to altar rails not to be alone; we Camino; we circle ancient places.

It's the time of year also, when other night-sky gazers are storied: Zoroastrian Magi who gathered themselves to follow another alignment, a sky-portent to herald the birth of a child-king. On a journey to 'The Light of the World.'

A time when the pursuit of the light moved from the outer to the inner realm. From study of the heavens to navigation of an inner Kingdom. A step-change in consciousness – to Inner Light.

But the journey, the pilgrimage there is not always smooth. As T. S. Eliot showed in 'The Journey of the Magi', through a hard winter with the voices singing 'folly' in their ears.

But it wasn't. Their part in a story scribing the Divine as Light, and Love. A candle lit to dress the darkness.

* * *

Mid-afternoon, North Belfast lies under a slate-grey sky, awaiting the gathering storm, and Brendan joins me to climb a wind-whipped Cavehill.

Between gulps of air, we talk of how the Camino forces you to live in the moment, especially when things go wrong. It might be when your wallet, pack or passport gets lost or stolen, or a sudden illness that casts you adrift in a strange land.

Then you have to stop, he says, and breathe through the descending chaos, however loudly your inner voice screams, and navigate the darkness until the tide turns. He speaks from experience. He has a patent-pending in disaster pilgrimage.

But back home in the everyday of a too-long winter, it's easier said than done.

* * *

At McArtt's Fort lookout a gull suddenly rises to stream away across this city in healing but not-yet-healed. And as the day leaves, colours glow in flats below that wealth has passed by; lights draped in hope and love, remembering a journey to a stall to be part of something bigger.

Often on December evenings, I imagine a presence brooding over these hills surrounding – from Castlereagh to Divis – cradling this city of separate development, of 'benign' apartheid. Where something new, full of contradictions, is birthing.

We turn from the gathering dark, make for a café and talk of family and of unrealistic expectations heightened by bright-lit shop windows.

The café's soundtrack plays Emmylou Harris's, *There's a Light in the Darkness*, with its promise that we all will fly. By and by.

As the rain smears windows, I mention that I saw Deacon Blue recently, playing *Raintown* in the Ulster Hall. 'It's a metaphor for something, I think.'

'Belfast in winter,' he says.

* * *

En route to Friday night Ravenhill Rugby, I wander through the City Centre Christmas Market, where, ten plus years ago, a Big Wheel spun out a candy-floss good fortune: of easy credit and rising house prices. Celtic Tigers leapt the Irish border and drove them higher still as lattes and frappuccinos filled bistro tables everywhere. Dickensian austerity decommissioned. Or so we thought.

Beneath the Ulster Hall's Edwardian canopy on Belfast's Dublin Road, blue light pulses from a CD player, its song drifting from a huddle of rough sleepers with foreign tongues who listen to 'Seasons Change,' another Will Regan/United Pursuit song from my days tracking the Rio Umia. Violin and piano figures raise the words, that despite such changes, Your love remains.[53]

But of course, *You* are here also, amongst the least; among these far travellers spat out in search of work or seeking shelter. Exposed as alone. At Christmas.

Have we not all committed that unforgivable sin? And carried the shame through crowds hoping no one will notice? Then thank God it's not *us exposed* tonight to the elements, flung from Hearth in search of Home, to take refuge under a canopy without walls; lacking any safe place to construct a sacred space.

What must that be like? To be so tested by the dark.

Might we yet welcome these wanderers?

Might they still find shelter, like Bede's sparrow, in the fleeting warmth of the Great Hall of feasting, passing from winter to winter? Or in the warmth of another swaddled child flung here from somewhere far, with his alien, brown-wet puppy eyes, burdened by hopes and fears but bringing the shelter of stories. Especially the one we learn huddled together, clung to mothers then each other – sung out in mid-winter welcome.

And even if they're not true, I'd still choose to believe them.

But tonight, I don't have the words. Only a few coins rendered, hardly enough to tip the scales to His side of the equation.

CHAPTER 31

Christmas Eve and St Jude's Parish Church, Belfast

The High Street of a North Down coastal town is abuzz this morning with charity Santas atop tractors, their klaxon horns fit for a second coming. Christmas jumpers are also out, tinsel wrapped, in queues outside butchers' or flitting in and out of un-shuttered shops: saddlers, greengrocers, jewellery and watch repairs, then bakers, hairdressers or 'Ice Creams to go'.

This street from another age has kept one-click purchasing at bay. For now. It's still a place of interaction, of social cohesion.

In the Co-op a man greeted with, 'You back already?' smilingly holds up a fluorescent tube and announces, 'I am the light.'

Everywhere relief and release is in the air – from the tyranny of the rush, or the trudge through storm, hail, or Belfast's crowded mean streets. Today the pleasure principle rules: touch-test the firmness of last-minute vegetables, or loiter over coffee observing others gather treasure.

The sky becomes bright above a town that knows all about stables, starry, starry nights of deep silence, and Story that restores order to chaos. High on gable walls, giant King James quotes echo out as reminder. This place now part of something bigger on the cusp of arrival. The memory of tonight and tomorrow will carry many through dark times.

Everywhere, stars, snowmen or desert travellers have been stencilled onto windows. Then Nature also puts on a display. On our way to the harbour, it seems as if a conjurer removes a rippling silk handkerchief to reveal a towering vault of sky burnished blue – into which seagulls soar above a low sun, their wing tips a luminous pink. Both the lighthouse and the whites of houses are aglow in this golden hour that will last all day. Light for the fleet to find its way home by, and for me also.

In the crackling air you can see for miles … past Ailsa Craig to a whaleback of Galloway coast rising, about tae blow. The world become a lustrous, wrap-around cinema screen.

Gulls cry, hung in the breeze. Like they always did when we lived by the sea, like they did ten miles north of Porto when other journeys started. We go to see new things, then perhaps see home with new eyes.

* * *

In the evening, I drive to Belfast where, under a star-bright sky, the gritter lorries cast their spray of pink hail clouds over frosted footpaths.

One Christmas Eve it snowed thick white flakes, each unique, fragile, sublime. Their stories like ours, carved onto their surface by the conditions of their descent to earth. But not tonight.

I drive-by my parents' first home to catch a trace of their dreams and carry them with me.

Everything looks smaller, less tall. But the lights are on. Blue LEDs pulse behind an angel outline and a star stuck to the window pane, complete with comet tail arcing across a glassy sky. Perhaps, inside, children again excited for tree presents.

On past the city's now silent tills where the bars have finally emptied. Leaving only strange-shaped buildings like St Jude's church open for late-night business; that of a counter-culture casting shadows of a different future, there with us in the agony of waiting.

St Jude's Parish Church: where I'd spent so many restless Sunday mornings as men in pulpits laboured to construct the architecture of belief. Jude and Caralampio, perhaps conjoined patron saints of seemingly lost causes, urging endurance.

Through a narrow porch, past lattice wood screens, I step into the candled half-light to hear again of hope arriving not as a military Messiah, but as a vulnerable babe first announced to the least of us. To the ritually unclean, outcast shepherds living their mundane lives on a frozen hillside, called to a place in which they'd feel at ease: a stinking Bethlehem stable. Invited to find a child as a gift, entrusted to the obscure and the poor, reversing the status of haves and have-nots.

The have-nots were now those lost in their temples, palaces, bordellos and board rooms – while the haves were lost in wonder … before a child of contradictions who'd turn over tables, then stand silent before accusers.

And for a moment I'm back in the Capilla San Pedro, Mouzos. Sitting with a Joseph forced back to his Bethlehem heartland, wondering what the heck to do now?

Could it really be to trust? Do the next thing? Take the next step?'

I bring the place names on a map once spoken like incantations – now become places in the heart: Labruge, Mt Trega, the Ria de Arousa, Armenteira, A Toxa, O Grove, Mouzos, Padron, The Rio Umia, A Corunna. Names I now silently mouth before an altar that I may divine their meaning along with others. Like Bethlehem or Nazareth. For in all weathers, across this spinning planet, similar little groups wander into strangely shaped buildings or gather round trees in clearings to listen to the same unlikely story, the one you'd never think to make up.

And if they're not at home, they still imagine themselves to be. For as travel writer Freya Stark wrote, 'Christmas... is not an external event at all, but a piece of home that we carry in our hearts'.

I am brought back to the present by the words of the liturgy 'You weigh not our merits but pardon our offences'. Words that bring an intense focus on the moment, and a heightened sense that someone knows everything about you, and sees every dark or wounded place, yet remains totally for you, loving you still. Someone familiar with wounds.

The priest exhorts us to take the communion cup 'and travel in our imagination tonight to Bethlehem – as *our* heartland also'. What else can we do? Who else has the words?

And as the line shuffles slowly towards the altar, the tired and old seemed, like in a Ribadumia dream, to become younger, straighter, taller; as if their inner child, brim-full with memories of nights like these, rose for a few moments to the surface, or felt close to a city whose gates shall never close.

I wait in line then, my turn come, kneel awkwardly at the rail, cupped hands extended, my Corrymeela wristband more ragged now but still glinting gold in the candlelight.

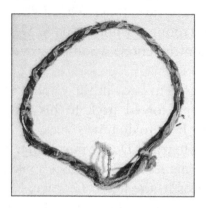

Corrymeela wristband

At the year's end the light returns. You can't sense it yet, but something is stirring, and not only in the plants and animals curled underground. The days and the story turns.

As we walk out into the air and before mystery recedes, Nature holds its breath as a greater silence arrives in solidarity with the new-born world.

For tonight, still, life is so good, so sharp and fresh that you can taste it in the very air.

* * *

The road home tracks the Lagan's eastward curve, the lights lining its far bank shimmer, doubled in the dark water beneath.

I turn away south, but the lights carry on and on, even when lost to sight as the river flows through the city's heart and into lough and sea. *Yet the sea is never full. Because to the place where the rivers rise, there they return to start again.*

St Patrick's Day 2020, Co. Down

I had to get away from all the noise, the anxiety rising. So I drove once more to the tidal island of Mahee and Nendrum's Monastic remains. Only to be reminded that its famous blackbird's song fell from a blackthorn (in Celtic culture a symbol of courage) enchanting Mo-Choi out of time, then returning him again to mediate between this and the Otherworld; joining a line stretched back to Tiresias.

Before long, the ash trees would burst into brilliance, as if lit from within, a time that usually signalled the start of the Camino season of long day's walking, set for a field of stars.

But not this year, when we came together by remaining apart.

So, I peered south, past Brigantia's tower towards another Celtic place on a map become a place in the heart. Where, atop Galicia's Mount Castrove, prayer daily rises in mediation. Between now and what may come next.

And with that, I somehow took heart, and drove again across the causeway, from one world back to another. But birdsong trailed my journey all the way home.

Notes

Chapter 3: Mount Trega (A Guarda)

1. The surname is interesting. On the one hand it refers to an Iron Age fortified hilltop settlement. It's also a common surname both here, in Latin America and in Cuba. Fidel Castro's father, 6Angel, was a Galician economic migrant.

2. A symbol familiar in Ireland, the Triskele, or triskelion (from Greek 'three-legged') consists of three bent human legs, or, more generally, three interlocked spirals. It's said to represent continuous movement forwards.

3. Newgrange is a World Heritage site ranked alongside the Pyramids of Gisa and Machu Picu.

Chapter 4: Celts, Seaborne Saints and a Pauline Protegee

4. They also kept livestock, sent out hunting parties, fished, gathered shellfish and mined the local mountains for tin, salt, or silver.

5. All our Eurasian languages seem to have a common root in 'Indo-European.'

6. When the relic of her right arm arrived from Armenia.

7. An ancient manuscript (the apocryphal Acts of Paul and Tecla) relates both her miraculous deliverance from martyrdom, and eventual retreat, as hermit and healer, to a cave in Silifke, now in south-central Turkey.

Chapter 7: Unearthing a Pilgrimage to Light

8. See the 'Book of Invasions', compiled by the eleventh-century to trace Irish history and purporting to show the Gaels arrival from Galicia.

9. Archaeologist Robert Hensey, in, 'First Light: The Origins of Newgrange,' corroborates it as a Pilgrimage site. He argues that if Newgrange hosted celebrations both at Solstice and Equinox, with people taking up one to two weeks for each, perhaps four to eight weeks of the year were being spent on pilgrim travels to and from Newgrange. Something mirrored in the Jewish people's journeys to and from Jerusalem three times a year. Though, by contrast, the Christian pilgrimage put greater stress on the journey than on arrival, as, the notion of 'The Kingdom of God is within you,' rather than a presence lodged in an external temple, gained greater currency.

Chapter 8: A Celtic Christianity Workshop and a Dream

10. See G. Clunie, 'Sacred Living: Practical Inspirations from Celtic Spirituality for the Contemporary Spiritual Journey'(2011), and G. Clunie and T. Maginness, 'The Celtic Spirit and Literature' (2015).

Chapter 10: Nendrum

11. Three hundred years was seen by Celts as a perfect unit of time, and Celtic tales often portrayed birds as angelic messengers, or creation unfallen.

12. There were no stone buildings here until the tenth century.

Chapter 14: O Grove

13. The Greek geographer Strabo documents how Galicia was once inhabited by tribes of Keltoi (the Greek word for Gaels).

Chapter 15: A Lanzada

14. The pagan Galician tradition of copulation upon special stones said to induce fertility – now sanitised to a prayer to The Virgin. The familiar Aphrodite symbology also ranges from a shell-shaped beach to foam as standing for semen.

15. The number nine was also linked to the sacred feminine and the months of pregnancy. The association of the number three with healing also occurs in Irish Mythology. When the Irish Goddess Cliodhna, goddess of love and beauty and Queen of the Banshees reportedly appeared at shorelines, she always has with her three birds whose song could cure ills. Those listening were sung to sleep and woke restored to health. The beneficial properties of saltwater are well known. Even today, some are still seduced into the sea in the hope that a ninth wave might bring healing or fertility.

16. Lebor Gabála Érenn (The Book of the Taking of Ireland), known in English as The Book of Invasions, is a collection of poems and prose compiled by the 11th Century intended as a history of Ireland and the Irish from the creation of the world to the Middle Ages. It tells how Ireland was settled (or 'taken') six times by various peoples. The final, sixth group, the Gaels, represent Ireland's current inhabitants.

17. It seems that agri-culture, trade and ideas, the Megalith and Passage Grave phenomena, art and cosmology seemed to flow like waves through these communities, bringing, I believe, a shared but not yet common culture, which provided a basement for development.

18. It seems possible that when copper and tin were merged to create Bronze Age swords and artefacts (2000-500 BC), the gaps in a shared culture were filled in to birth a more coherent 'Celtic' era – one that absorbed, not obliterated the past: just as the symbols atop Trega were lifted from the Neolithic period and repurposed. Even though the pioneers passed underground (like the De Daanan) their legacy remained as part of this composite culture.

Chapter 16: A Coruña and a Tower with a View

19. Immrama refers to a medieval Irish literary genre charting supernatural sea voyages motivated by religious reasons to miraculous islands.

20. The Journey of San Amaro is modelled on Brendan's ninth-century Navagatio text (though probably from and earlier tradition according to Monica Weiss) and incorporates elements of other Immrama stories: The Voyage of Bran in the seventh century, and of Maelduin, from the eighth. It also incorporates elements of the Legends of Mo-Choi/Ero. See Chapters 10 and 23.

21. In another version instead of going to Ireland, he sees the great 'Isle of Solstice' consecrated to Saint Thecla, a place where there is no hunger, pain or fear. See Chapter 4.

22. Their National Anthem hails Galicia as the home of Breogan – evidence that their preference for a Celtic origin continues.

23. The Irish regularly comprise the highest number of pilgrims per percentage of population.

24. It was here that provisions were marshalled for a real invasion – of Britannia, in 43 BC.

25. As are the many churches that appeared on Galicia's coast, from the fifth to the ninth century. Conversation with author, May 2019.

26. 'Pseudo History' often fills in the blanks of the skewed 'Proto Histories' written by Greek and Roman conquerers with a view to stressing their martial might.

27. The Book of Invasions tells the story of an honourable, poetic warrior people, who, despite suffering wrong (Ith's murder), did not merely seek revenge, but sought a solution through a water test, so to speak, an appeal to a higher power. Endorsed by the Divine as worthy inheritors of the land, they are brought to shore and, with right on their side, fight with ferocious fury, modelling out a pattern for future behaviour.

28. After the eighth-century the tower becomes less lighthouse and more fortress-lookout point to scan the sea for Viking raiders or invaders – the inhabitants retreating inland until Reconquista gathers pace in the thirteenth century and Alphonso 1X ordered its repopulation – Brigantium becoming Corunna.

29. Nationality then Nationalism originates when people marshal every possible resource to make a case for distinctness, banding together, an Us against a Them, in completion for scarce resources. This resource could be language, religion, skin tone or any physical distinctness. And it's always contested.

30. In Pursuit of Spring (1913).

31. See J. Carey, in *A Single Ray of Sun* (1999), p. 11.

32. This new form of worship which arrived in Ireland in the fifth century A.D. had monks setting out by boat on pilgrimages in search of solitude to contemplate the Divine, or a place of service. A practice especially appealing to an island people acquainted with boats, salt and sail.

Chapter 17: The Santiago Church by the Port

33. An era brought to an end by Reformation and conflict between England and Spain.

Chapter 18: Waterville, Ballinskelligs Bay, Co. Kerry

34. Lodestone meant 'Way Stones.' Later we were propelled by 'Trade Winds.' Trade referring to path or track.

35. Amergin's name, meaning 'Birth of Song,' infers a landscape that looks like a Hog's Head; Lough Ligda is linked with his wife Skena's burial, and Don, his brother, is reported as buried on Little Skellig Michael.

36. See: 'Amergin-Unde Scribitur' P. Bushe et al 2018. Amergin Solstice Poetry Gathering.

37. Conceivably, these later invasions (with a male to female ratio of twenty to one) might better account for the ubiquitous violence in the Irish Mythological Cycle. See Ulster Archeological Society Lecture, QUB, Jan 2020.

38. See Harbour Faith Community blogpost: https://harbourfaith.com/blog/2018/9/11/more-than-sand

Chapter 22: What We Choose to Remember – or Forget

39. For the Irish were regarded, in Count Caracena's words, as, 'The 'Spanish of the North,' grown from the same root, again referencing the myth of a Galician Celtic invasion in pre-history.

Chapter 23: The Stone and the Story – Armenteira and Nendrum

40. Ramon's contribution to Galician Literature was later commemorated with statues in Pontevedra and in Santiago where, in Alameda Park, he's seated contentedly, gazing forever across to the Cathedral.

41. I later learned that a similar version was attached to the founding of the ninth-century Cistercian Monastery of Leira (also in Navarre, about fifty kilometres east of Alloz). The story became the Legend of Abbot Saint Virila, before travelling east to Armenteira. This time it's Virilia who rambled in adjoining woods to meditate on eternal life. Drawn into a deep forest by a nightingale's song, he drinks from a crystal-clear fountain and sleeps. Waking, he returns to a much-enlarged monastery to be learn that St Virilia disappeared … again 300 years previously.

42. Such a compelling metaphor that it was replicated in the later San Amaro and Trezonzonia myths. See Ch.16. For Millenia, stories as well as goods were traded back and forth along Atlantic coastlines, so myth-making became guide, revelling in the power of Story to reveal a truth, behaving much like the writer of John's Gospel did: more interested in metaphor than linear narrative.

Chapter 24: The Rio Umia – River of Dreams, Memories

43. Asclepius' staff, with a serpent coiled about it, remains the symbol of the medical profession. And the Hebrew-Christian tradition records the Exodus serpent on the pole Moses lifted up in the desert. In both cases the shedding of skins symbolises renewal and healing.

44. https://www.youtube.com/watch?v=5PKsrucumYk

Chapter 26: The Island of Cortegada

45. The Rastro cage rake is a long pole with rake-teeth , fitted with a metal cage into which the shellfish fall.

46. The curved bow and deep keel of the Dorna is used on the open seas.

Chapter 28: Remembrance and Mount Santiaguiño, Padron

47. Though see The Guardian article 30/8/20: 'How Angela Merkel's Great Migrant Gamble paid off.' Her popularity has rebounded while the AFD's has stagnated.

Chapter 29: Kilbroney, a C.S. Lewis Window and a Celtic Worldview

48. Elsewhere, he explicitly references the 'Sons of Thunder' James and John, and their willingness to 'call down fire on a Samaritan village'.

49. The Tain describes a cattle raid involving Cuchulainn and Queen Meave of Connaught.

50. Perhaps it was this site that inspired Aslan's famous table and the wicked snow queen.

51. Perhaps it was this site that inspired Aslan's famous table and the wicked snow queen.

Chapter 30: Belfast, 14th December

52. See her book: The Natural Health Service.

53. https://www.youtube.com/watch?v=F7k5pqBVinA

Acknowledgements

Thanks to:
Grace Clunie for inspiration at the start of this journey.
Georgina Hatch for editing and encouragement.
Maria Seco of *Spanish for the Camino* for reviewing and improving the sections set in Spain.
Niki Boucher for beautiful maps.
Susan Jagannath for expertise, energy and encouragement.

For permissions to quote and assistance:
Professor John Carey.
Professor Geraldine Stout.
José Sáchez Pardo.
Group for the Study of Irish Historic Settlement.
Paddy Bushe and The Amergin Poetry Festival.
Thomas McErlean.
Steve Ames and Harbour Faith Community.

Free Bonus Content

If you'd like to receive a free PDF with more photos of places in the book, you can email Roy at: uprichard.roy@gmail.com

Also by Roy Uprichard:
Restless Hearts – Walking the Camino de Santiago
Stone & Water – Walking the Spiritual Variant of the Camino Portugués
Piedra Y Agua – Andando por la Variante Espiritual del Camino Portugués (Spanish Edition of *Stone & Water*)

All available as e-books and print books on Amazon.

Note to Readers

Dear Reader,
If you enjoyed reading this book – please review and share it. It will help others find it.
I'd really appreciate that.

Just go to amazon.co.uk or amazon.com, enter my name and/or the book title in the search box, scroll down to *Customer Reviews*, then click on *Write a Customer Review*.

Thank you,
Roy

You can also email me at: uprichard.roy@gmail.com. It would be great to know your impressions. It would mean a lot. And help the writing.

About the Author

Roy Uprichard was born in Belfast, and, as a mature student graduated from Queen's University and went into teaching. Prior to that, he had to work for a living.

In 2010, in a partially successful assault on middle-age-spread, he trekked part of the Annapurna circuit in Nepal and began to write. The Himalayas must share responsibility for this.

Their peaks then led to the flatter mountains of the Camino Francés, and he left teaching to become an author, wine-taster and Camino enthusiast who loves to share his experiences with those who cannot walk.

His latest passion is exploring on (and off) the various routes of the Camino Portugués, and their Celtic connections with home in Ireland.

He lives in North Down and hopes to continue walking, writing and wine-tasting.

Also by Roy Uprichard

***Restless Hearts** – Walking the Camino de Santiago* **(2016)**
An emotional and spiritual journey across Spain.

In an evocative mix of travel writing and memoir, an Irish pilgrim fallen out of love with his Church yet finds himself drawn to walk the Camino de Santiago. Deeply moved by encounters with other restless hearts, he begins to find his way again.

Review by the Confraternity of St James, London:
'More than a memoir. A reflection on life, belief and non-belief, by one of the many restless hearts wrapped in a temporary pilgrim mantle, seeking to regain their land of lost content. Full of vivid description and capturing those fleeting impressions that bring an experience alive.'

Some of the 5-star reviews of Restless Hearts on Amazon:

'I recommend this without hesitation. Packed with details and poetry, it will lift your soul. This beautiful book invites the reader to join in the author's journeys, both physical and spiritual.'

'Would recommend to anyone wanting to get an insight into the Camino.'

'Fantastic book for anybody who has, or indeed hasn't experienced the Camino. You feel as if you too are walking with him, bathed in the sunlight of the experience. The immediate challenges and experiences of the Camino trigger the author's memories of long forgotten incidents so that we have walked through many different layers of history by the time we reach our destination at Santiago de Compostella.'

'Restless Hearts is a book I'd recommend to anyone. There are the poet and the artist's hand in this book. The prose is beautiful, he paints a picture of history, both past and present, both entertaining and informative. The interactions with people along the way, the friendships gained that will last a lifetime. I found the book a page turner and reasonably priced. A great present for anyone with a restless heart.'

'A wonderful account of a personal, spiritual and historical journey. Well worth the read.'

'I loved the mixture of travel writing and memories evoked on the walk, the authors reference to making sense of the past and how the Camino brings to the surface things previously buried or denied. I particularly enjoyed the author's recollections of his early life and his search for information about his father. I feel inspired to do this walk and experience the scenery, the people, the light and the villages along the way. Lovely descriptions of all this.'

'This is more than a travelogue but an honest and personal account of how given the opportunity the Camino can impact the searching pilgrim. Thank you Roy.'

Stone & Water – Walking the Spiritual Variant of the Camino Portugués (2017)

A walk through hidden Galicia on the trail of saints and scholars.

In August 2016 I walked north from Porto on the Camino Portugués, to Santiago de Compostela. The route that made the deepest impression came just after Pontevedra: The Spiritual Variant, or Stone and Water Route, added to the Camino itinerary in 2013.

Its meditative paths led me through a region of lavish fertility; of vineyards and green pastures; of forested hillsides, remote glens and living waters. By following it, I discovered a place of history, myth and Celtic resonance with Ireland.

'A magical journey out of time and into silence, peace and beauty. Bursting with lyrical phrases and pictures.'

'A deeply meaningful book for any Camino journey.'

Some of the 5-star reviews of *Stone & Water* on Amazon
'This is much more than a travel guide. It is a story of people met along the way, the connections between Christianity, myth and literature. Roy's prose is full of delicious poetic phrases. Such a delighted read that I devoured it in 2 sunny days!'

'We only found out about the Spiritual Variant when we arrived in Arcade. The owner of the Hostel almost insisted we take this route. So glad we did. It was the best part of our journey. Wish we had read your book first. It would have provided so much more insight. Reading it brought back great memories and put a lot of context around what we had seen and what we missed. Would love to do this segment of the Camino again.'

'Anyone planning to walk the Camino Portuguese, should read this.'

'This a short book but filled with colourful descriptions of the towns trails the author walked. What I liked best about the book was his weaving of history and myth into the story of his journey. I was looking for a book about the Portuguese Camino but got much more than that. I have read many books about the Camino that describe the trials of walking. This went much deeper in his thoughts and insights. I can highly recommend this book for any one thinking of walking any Camino to get a taste of how you might change from the experience or to veteran walkers wanting to rekindle the feelings of the trail.'

'If you want to take a trip on a magical journey out of time and into silence, peace and beauty, you couldn't do better than read Roy Uprichard's second book, Stone & Water. Bursting with lyrical phrases and pictures, like a vine full of ripe fruit, this is a book to read, enjoy, and then reread time and again. I particularly love Chapter

Five, which describes the part of the walk called the route of Stone and Water. 'Steep steps take me from one world into the cool of another, the mystic heart of this walk...A chorus in the mystery play of water's circular motion.' The pun of 'mystery play' highlights the spiritual layer of the writing; and later, in Chapter Nine, Uprichard's thoughts about C S Lewis's views on the underlying truth in the pagan myths of death and resurrection, fulfilled in the incarnation, death and resurrection of Christ, are a further cause for reflection. From blisters and meals of seafood to awe inspiring views and buildings, not forgetting the fellow pilgrims met along the way, this book is firmly underpinned by reality, and yet manages to lift us out of the mundane into the mystical beauty of creation. Give yourself a real treat by buying this. I couldn't recommend it more enthusiastically.'

'With upwards of a quarter of a million walking or riding the Camino Frances each year, many returning pilgrims are seeking to both explore other ways of arriving and to deepen their reflective experiences. Roy's second Camino book – after his successful Restless Hearts – does just this in giving an uplifting account of the 3-day Spiritual Variant that was added to the Camino in 2013.'

'I enjoyed going with Roy on what he has described as 'new conversations on the way to a Galician Emmaus'. I hope to do it soon in a concrete way with this book (including its tailored information sources) as my guide and stimulus.'

And, to improve one's Spanish:

Piedra Y Agua: Andando por la Variante Espiritual del Camino Portugués (Spanish Edition of Stone & Water) 2018